Clever Girl Finance, My Wealth Plan Workbook

Clever Girl Finance, My Wealth Plan Workbook

Your Personalized Plan to Ditch Debt, Save Money and Build Real Wealth

Bola Sokunbi

WILEY

Published by John Wiley & Sons, Inc., Hoboken, New Jersey.
Published simultaneously in Canada.

For general information on our other products and services or for technical support, please contact our Customer Care Department within the United States at (800) 762-2974, outside the United States at (317) 572-3993 or fax (317) 572-4002.

Wiley also publishes its books in a variety of electronic formats. Some content that appears in print may not be available in electronic formats. For more information about Wiley products, visit our web site at www.wiley.com.

Library of Congress Cataloging-in-Publication Data is Available:

ISBN 9781394266913 (Paperback)
ISBN 9781394266920 (epdf)
ISBN 9781394266937 (epub)

Cover Design: Wiley
Cover Image: Courtesy of Clever Girl Finance

SKY10086721_100424

Contents

Contents

Contents

About the Author

Bola Sokunbi is a Certified Financial Education Instructor (CFEI), investor, finance expert, speaker, podcaster, bestselling author, and the founder and CEO of Clever Girl Finance, one of the largest personal finance media/education platforms for women in the U.S.

She is the recipient of the 2021 Financial Education Instructor of the Year (FEIY) Award from the National Council of Financial Educators (NFEC). Clever Girl Finance has also earned the Distinguished Personal Finance Content (DPFC) designation from the National Financial Educators Council, having proven competency in providing financial education that aligns with industry best practices and research-based education principles.

Based on her experience saving over $100,000 in three and a half years after graduating from college and navigating through various financial mistakes and successes of her own in the years that followed, Bola started Clever Girl Finance in 2015 to provide women with the tools and resources she wished she had when she began her financial journey.

She lives with her husband and twins in New Jersey.

Also by Bola Sokunbi

Clever Girl Finance: Ditch Debt, Save Money, and Build Real Wealth

Learn How Investing Works, Grow Your Money

The Side Hustle Guide: Build a Successful Side Hustle and Increase Your Income

Choosing to Prosper: Triumphing Over Adversity, Breaking Out of Comfort Zones, Achieving Your Life and Money Dreams

Acknowledgments

I'm so glad to have been able to create this amazing workbook, and I couldn't have done it without the support and love from so many of the wonderful people in my life.

First off, a huge thank-you to my wonderful husband. Your constant support and belief in me have kept me going, even when things got tough. To my beautiful twins, your laughter and love inspire me to be the best version of myself every day.

To my dear sister-friends, thank you for your endless encouragement, late-night chats, and for always being there to cheer me on. You've been my sounding board and my biggest cheerleaders.

To my mentors, your wisdom and guidance have been invaluable. You've helped me navigate the complexities of the business world and have taught me so much along the way.

To team CGF, thank you for always holding the fort down with every book project, for your insights, and for all your support. There would be no Clever Girl Finance without you.

And to the incredible women in the Clever Girl Finance community – you are all *so* amazing! Your stories of resilience and determination have inspired me beyond words. The Clever Girl Finance book series and this new workbook draw from the collective wisdom of this fantastic community.

My hope for this workbook is that it becomes a trusted companion on your financial journey, that it inspires you to lay out your financial goals clearly, and that it empowers you to take action toward achieving them. Let this be your stepping-stone to financial independence, wealth building, and creating the life you've always dreamed of.

Here's to your journey to financial greatness!

Welcome to Your Wealth Plan Workbook!

Thank you for picking up your very own wealth plan workbook! I'm so excited to be right here with you as you embark on this transformative journey toward your success, one that will reshape your life in a profound and incredible way.

If you've already read the *Clever Girl Finance* book series, you'll find that this workbook is the perfect companion to build upon the foundation you've already begun creating. If you're new to *Clever Girl Finance* and this is the first book you've picked up, this is an excellent starting point that contains everything you need to start making your dreams a reality.

Created specifically for women like you, this workbook is a hands-on resource to help you get clear on your financial and life goals and then translate them into actionable steps you can immediately start taking toward your dreams and desires.

Whether you're just starting your financial journey, are looking to refine your existing strategies, or are starting over (no shame!), you'll get the tools and guidance you need to create the life you truly desire for yourself and on your own terms – because "Why not you?!"

This workbook is perfect for you if:

- You're tired of feeling overwhelmed or uncertain about your financial situation.
- You want to pay off debt, save money, invest to build wealth, and pursue financial independence.
- You're looking for hands-on, practical resources that you can apply directly to your life along with a structured framework to help you streamline managing your money.
- You're eager to advance in your career or business, explore new opportunities, and make strategic decisions about your professional development and life in general.
- You're committed to your personal growth and empowerment and are ready to act and make positive changes in your life.

I'll be guiding you through a comprehensive set of exercises, checklists, and worksheets that I have crafted based on principles I teach through the Clever Girl Finance platform. These principles have already helped thousands of women and have been compiled here to support you at every stage of this growth journey you'll be embarking on. We'll be ditching complexity, and instead you'll gain clarity and confidence about the steps you need to take to achieve not just your financial goals, but your personal goals as well.

Together we will:

- Dive deep into your mindset and beliefs with dedicated exercises to help you reflect on your relationship with money, to identify areas for growth and improvement, and to define your core values.
- Organize your financial records, create a realistic budget, develop debt repayment strategies, and outline savings and investment plans tailored to your goals and aspirations.
- Create strategies for improving your financial health, excelling in your career, and building or growing your side hustle and pursuing your life goals.
- Reflect on your progress and document your journey with dedicated journaling areas that will allow you to celebrate your wins and learn from your challenges, as you chart your course toward your success.

The *Clever Girl Finance Workbook* is more than just a companion – it's your roadmap to financial empowerment. With its practical tools, insightful exercises, and actionable guidance, this workbook will empower you to take control of your finances and build the life you envision.

So get ready to embark on a transformative journey towards your financial freedom. It's time for you to start building wealth, one smart decision at a time!

How to Use This Workbook

This workbook is essentially your personalized plan to achieve your financial goals. To make sure you get the most out of this workbook as you create your wealth plan, here are some key tips:

- This workbook is split into four sections. You can dive into any section you like first, but each section is meant to be done in order. So if you start with a particular section, aim to finish all its subsections in sequence.
- Set aside dedicated time to work without distractions. This will help you stay focused and committed to your goals.
- Before diving into the exercises, take some time to envision your ideal future. Having a vision will motivate and guide you as you work through this workbook. Don't worry about the specifics as you think through your vision; that's what this workbook is here to help you detail!
- If you feel you already have a section of the workbook covered, or you want to come back to it later, it's okay to skip ahead. Focus on what's relevant to you right now.

- Be honest and transparent with yourself about your current financial situation, goals, and challenges. Transparency is key to creating a realistic and effective wealth plan, and no one else needs to see this workbook but you.
- Don't just complete the exercises and fill out the worksheets. Commit to taking action and use the plans you create in this workbook as your personal action guide. Be intentional about implementing the plans you create on a consistent basis so you can move closer to achieving your goals.
- Review your completed entries regularly to track your progress. Celebrate your wins and identify areas for improvement to stay motivated and on track.
- Understand that your financial situation and goals may evolve over time. Be open to adjusting your wealth plan as needed to reflect changes in your life circumstances or priorities. If you change your mind about certain things, that's okay too.
- Finally, use a pencil or an erasable pen so you can make corrections or edits.

Remember, this workbook is a tool to help you take control of your financial future. By following these tips and staying committed to the process, you'll be well on your way to building wealth and making your dreams of financial freedom a reality.

For additional resources, visit clevergirlfinance.com to check out our completely free personal finance courses and participate in our amazing community. To download printable pdf and Excel versions of worksheets in this workbook, visit clevergirlfinance.com/my-wealth-plan.

Committing to Yourself: The Clever Girl Finance Creed

Before you begin, I invite you to make a personal commitment to this process. By signing and dating the creed below, you are affirming your dedication to taking the necessary actions, embracing any challenges, and staying the course.

Your success starts with this promise to yourself, and your dedication and perseverance will play a crucial role in transforming your financial future!

The Clever Girl Finance Creed

I, _____,
commit to actively engaging with this workbook, implementing the strategies and lessons it provides, and taking the necessary steps to achieve my financial goals. I understand that this journey requires dedication, effort, and persistence, and I am fully committed to seeing it through.

I pledge to:

- Consistently allocate time to work through each section of this workbook, understanding that steady progress is key to achieving my financial goals.
- Approach this journey with an open mind, eager to learn and apply new financial concepts, strategies, and skills.
- Actively implement the advice and steps outlined in this workbook, making tangible changes to my financial habits and behaviors.
- Acknowledge that there may be challenges and setbacks along the way, but I will stay committed to my financial journey, using these obstacles as opportunities to learn and grow.
- Seek advice or assistance when needed, understanding that collaboration and support can enhance my journey toward financial success.
- Recognize and celebrate my achievements, no matter how small, because each step forward is a vital part of my financial transformation.

Signature: _____

Workbook Completion Checklist

Use this checklist as a reference and to track your progress through the sections of this workbook:

Check the box next to each section or subsection as you complete them.

☐	**Part 1: Financial Foundations**
☐	• Your Money Story
☐	• Letting Go of Your Money Mistakes
☐	• Dream Big: Affirming Yourself to Wealth
☐	• Shifting Your Circle of Influence
☐	• Getting Your Financial Records in Order
☐	• Tracking Your Spending
☐	• Breaking Up with Your Bad Money Habits
☐	• Your Net Worth
☐	• Your Core Values
☐	• Your Financial (and Life) Goals

(continued)

- ☐ • Your Budget
- ☐ • Paying Down Your Debt (Credit Cards, Student Loans, etc.)
- ☐ • Your Credit
- ☐ • Protecting Yourself (Insurance)
- ☐ • Asking for More Money
- ☐ • Your Self-Care

☐ **Part 2: Investing**

- ☐ • Your Investing Mindset
- ☐ • Preparing to Invest
- ☐ • Researching Your Investments
- ☐ • Making Your Investments
- ☐ • Investing for Retirement
- ☐ • Checking In on Your Investments

☐ **Part 3: Side Hustles**

- ☐ • Preparing for a Side Hustle
- ☐ • Laying Out Your Business Idea
- ☐ • Beginning Your Business Plan
- ☐ • Branding and Marketing Your Business
- ☐ • Your Business Finances
- ☐ • Business Metrics to Track
- ☐ • Your Dream Team

☐ **Part 4: Choosing to Prosper**

- ☐ • Making the Intentional Choice to Prosper
- ☐ • Who You Are
- ☐ • Coming of Age
- ☐ • Your Career Journey
- ☐ • Taking Leaps of Faith
- ☐ • Empowering Others Despite the Naysayers
- ☐ • Choosing a Rich Partner
- ☐ • Stepping Outside Your Comfort Zone
- ☐ • Beating Imposter Syndrome
- ☐ • Celebrating Yourself
- ☐ • Intentionally Choosing to Prosper Moving Forward

Clever Girl Finance, My Wealth Plan Workbook

PART I

Financial Foundations

CHAPTER **1**

Your Money Story

Our experiences with money and the financial role models we had growing up can be vastly different. Perhaps you had certain financial privileges, or maybe your family always faced financial struggles. Regardless of your background, both the positive and negative aspects of your financial story play a significant role in shaping your current relationship with money. And so, to achieve a positive and fulfilling relationship with your finances, it's essential to reflect on your financial history and confront any money-related obstacles directly.

So what's your money story?

This first exercise will help you get clear on how your past and your upbringing ties into your relationship with money today. Take some time to write down your responses to the questions below about your history as it relates to money, and your current financial attitudes and behaviors. Be as detailed and honest as possible in your answers.

Why this exercise is important: Understanding your money story will help you see where you struggle and what causes your anxiety and worry about money. You want to make sure that as you start working on your wealth plan, you address any roadblocks from your history with money, so you can get comfortable about where you are headed with your finances.

What did you learn about money from your parents or parental figures based on how they managed their finances?

If you were aware of money matters or financial challenges in your household growing up, how did you feel?

What were the positives or negatives about money in your life when you were growing up?

What's the one money memory or emotional experience tied to money you have from growing up that's stuck with you to this day?

How do you think this money memory or emotional experience affects the way you deal with money today?

Were there any specific financial rules or values that your parents or other family members instilled in you?

What about money makes you anxious or stressed?

Read over your answers and reflect on your thoughts and feelings about what you've written. Once you've done a thorough reflection, write down the money roadblocks your currently face today and one to three key actions you can take to overcome these roadblocks as well as assign timeframes over the next few days and months to start taking action.

Here are some examples of roadblocks as well as ideas of actions you can take:

- *Roadblock:* **Your family did not speak about money openly.**
    If your family didn't discuss money openly, you might have some financial literacy gaps and you might avoid your finances altogether.
    - *Action:* Create a plan to improve your financial literacy (you are already on the right path!) and consistently empower yourself with knowledge. Seek support from a certified financial professional like a counselor or therapist if necessary. No shame, no judgment.
- *Roadblock:* **You've always spent money without a plan.**
    If you grew up in an environment where spending was encouraged or not monitored, you might struggle with overspending.
    - *Action:* Explore various budgeting methods, start tracking your expenses, and start practicing mindful/intentional spending.
- *Roadblock:* **You were taught to fear investing.**
    If your family avoided investing due to fear or a lack of understanding, you might hesitate to invest.
    - *Action:* Start learning how investing works, start small, and focus on broad diversification.

- *Roadblock:* **Your family was always in debt.**

  If you grew up in a household where debt was the norm, you might also normalize debt or struggle with managing it.
  - *Action:* Create a debt repayment plan to start tackling your existing debt head on and be intentional about avoiding new debt.
- *Roadblock:* **You have a negative money mindset.**

  If your upbringing instilled negative beliefs in your mind about money like "money is hard to get" or "rich people are greedy," you may have been self-sabotaging your own financial progress due to this mindset.
  - *Action:* Identify your limiting beliefs and write them out. Then challenge them by replacing them with positive and empowering ones.
- *Roadblock:* **You did not grow up around financial goals.**

  If your family didn't set financial goals or prioritize savings, you might struggle with doing this yourself.
  - *Action:* Lay out the specific financial goals you'd like to achieve and a savings plan for each one.

Roadblocks	Key actions to address roadblocks	Specific dates to take action by (Set a reminder on your calendar)

Roadblocks	Key actions to address roadblocks	Specific dates to take action by (Set a reminder on your calendar)

Remember, recognizing these patterns is the first step toward breaking free. By acknowledging and addressing them, you can develop healthier financial habits and achieve financial stability.

Unsure about how to take specific action? Don't worry, there are several action tasks and exercises throughout this workbook that can help you challenge various roadblocks you might be experiencing. So keep going!

Your *Why*

As you work on building wealth it's super-important to focus on having a plan for emergencies, learning to budget, paying off debt, having savings goals, and investing – but before you start making those plans, it's important to have the right mindset and focus in place.

If you aren't quite sure, **your *why* is essentially the driving force that keeps you going, especially when life starts *life-ing* and everything in you wants to quit.** It provides you with a sense of direction and is tied to your purpose, which in turn ties into you living a fulfilled life. It can also help you overcome your fears and doubts because you'll be reminded of your purpose, which is bigger than any fear or doubt you might have.

Finding your *why* is about being honest with yourself and getting clear on what truly makes you happy and the deeper motivation that causes you to want certain things in your life. It should be the reason for the goals you choose to pursue.

Keep in mind that you can have multiple *why*s. You can even have a *why* associated with different aspects of your life, like your family and relationships, your career, your health and wellness, your personal growth, and, of course, your finances.

For example, when it comes to the goals you have that are tied to your family and relationships, your *why* might be to create beautiful and long-lasting memories, spend quality time together, and cultivate deeper connections and emotional intimacy.

Your *why* in your career might be to make a positive impact through the work that you do, find fulfillment through work, and be a strong leader in your field that inspires others.

For your health and wellness, your *why* might be to improve your mental and emotional well-being, improve your physical fitness, and reduce stress and overwhelm in your life.

For your personal growth, it might be to continue to develop and improve on specific skills, build up your self-confidence and communication skills, cultivate mindfulness, and grow a deeper sense of self.

Now when it comes to your finances, it's important that you really spend the time to lay out your *why*. This is because your finances pretty much touch every aspect of your life in one way or another. While not the sole factor, money is a key contributor to:

- The quality of life you live with your family and the experiences you have
- Your ability to acquire the education and skills needed for a career path
- Improving your health and wellness through access to good nutrition, good healthcare, a good living environment, and more

And so, with that said, your *why* (or *why*s) when it comes to money might include:

- Creating financial security and stability for you and your family so you don't have to worry about money
- Becoming debt free
- Starting your own business to expand your earning potential
- Being able to fund travel to create new experiences
- Retiring early to enjoy more of life while you are still young and healthy
- Building generational wealth for your children and their children
- Giving back financially to positively impact the life of others in your family, community, or through charitable endeavors

Now that you know what a *why* is and why having one is so important, ask yourself, "Why do I want to succeed with my finances?" This will involve you doing some serious reflection and might take some time, but it's an important step you don't want to skip.

Your *why* is personal to you. It's not about what other people expect you to want, what society's standards are, or who your Instagram or TikTok feed says you should be. It's about what truly matters to you and what brings you fulfillment.

It's important to keep in mind that your *why* may also change or evolve over time as you navigate different life stages and experiences. This is normal and if it happens to you, it's okay. Personally, my *why* has changed several times from when I was single and it was all about me, to when I got married and I added on new joint *why*s with my husband, to when I became a mother and adjusted some of my *why*s based on the legacy we want to create for our children.

As human beings, we are constantly growing and evolving, so if you feel a shift in what drives you and gives you fulfillment, adjust your *why* accordingly.

Your *why* will also tie into establishing your core values, which we'll delve into in more detail a little later.

As you go on this journey to financial wellness, it's inevitable that you will face challenges and setbacks. However, regardless of what challenges or setbacks you may face, making up your mind that "you can" and establishing your *why* is the foundation of what will keep you motivated to put in the effort.

You'll have to come up with ideas to make things work. You'll have to do things that might not necessarily be ideal. You may make mistakes along the way. But as long as you lean on your ability, are aware of your *why*, and are not afraid to fail, and as long as you understand that within every failure is a lesson that can propel you forward, you can do whatever you put your mind to.

But first you have to want your financial success, however you choose to define it, badly enough. Now, let's define your *why*.

What it is you want to accomplish with your finances and other aspects of your life?

Why do you want to accomplish it? What is your *why*?
(Remember, you can have multiple *why*s.)

Make a copy of your *why* (or *why*s) from this workbook and put it somewhere you'll see it every day as a constant reminder of why you need to succeed. Be sure to carve out time to reflect on your *why* periodically.

CHAPTER **2**

Letting Go of Your Money Mistakes

Like me, you've probably made a few or (*cough*) several money mistakes. But now you're here, and you've made the decision that you can be financially successful, and the good news is that you can! That said, you are going to have to work on developing your mindset to keep it in top shape, just like you would any other muscle in your body, and part of that work is letting go of your money mistakes.

So here are three steps you can take right now to help you let go of your money mistakes, so you can start making real progress toward your goals.

1. Acknowledge your mistakes and forgive yourself.

To get ahead, you are going to have to forgive yourself for your money mistakes, take the lessons you've learned, and keep it moving.

Yes, mistakes happen. Everyone has made bad decisions around their money – even the world's wealthiest people. I can guarantee that any well-known wealthy person you can think of has made at least one major mistake with their money at some point on their financial journey. Mistakes are part of the learning process in life, and they provide you with an opportunity to grow.

So acknowledge where you went wrong, take ownership, figure out what to do to make things right (on your own or with the right support), and end the self-judgment. It's time to move forward and let go of any resentment or guilt you are feeling. The pity party is over.

Even if you wind up making the same or similar mistakes again (mistakes are inevitable), give yourself grace. Your approach should be to rinse and repeat the process of acknowledging the mistake, learning how to improve, and implementing the lessons until you get past your error.

2. Decide it's time to take action toward change.

Next, you have to be willing to change and be committed to seizing the moment to start working on revamping your finances, right now. No more waiting for perfect – the perfect job, the perfect city, the perfect relationship. Just start.

This means creating a plan to address any consequences or setbacks because of your past mistakes and setting clear and achievable goals.

This also means that if you can only save $5 a week right now, save that $5. It means that if you can only put $10 toward your debt this week, make that $10 payment until you get to the point where you are able to ramp it up. It's less about the amount and more about the consistent action.

3. Get motivated.

When you start working on your financial goals, there will be a period of euphoria. You'll get that fresh sense of excitement that comes with new goals. However, as you go through the motions of accomplishing your goals and as time goes by, you are going to need continuous motivation to help you stay focused. That's what will keep you going when it comes to the things you want to achieve in your life, and you have to be mindful of where you seek it.

Some ways to stay motivated include finding an accountability partner, reading books, working on this workbook, listening to podcasts, or watching videos that keep you excited as you make progress on your financial goals.

That said, it's time to work through your past mistakes, take the lessons, and bid them bye-bye!

Make a list of every money mistake you've made that you can think of and write out the lessons you can take away from each mistake.

Money mistakes	Lessons learned

Money mistakes	Lessons learned

Now, take a deep breath, forgive yourself, and let it go.
Repeat after me:

I forgive myself for my money mistakes.
I accept the lessons.
I let that ish go.

Scream it out loud if necessary – it works wonders, I promise!

Now it's time to make a list of ways you can stay motivated, books you can read, podcasts you can listen to, video series you can watch, and people you can connect with.

Set a timeframe to start working through this list.

Motivation list (To do, to read, to listen to, to watch, to connect with)	Specific dates to take action by (Set a reminder on your calendar)

Motivation list (To do, to read, to listen to, to watch, to connect with)	Specific dates to take action by (Set a reminder on your calendar)

CHAPTER 3

Dream Big: Affirming Yourself to Wealth

Personally, I'm a huge fan of affirmations. They help me get my head in the game and they serve as reminders of my *why*. I use affirmations in my day-to-day life around my financial goals, my business goals, my fitness goals, and other life goals I want to accomplish. They provide emotional support and encouragement as I make progress, and they are essentially another form of motivation for me.

But what exactly is an affirmation? Well, to put it simply, **an affirmation is declaring something to be true.** When you declare or affirm something, you are in conscious control of your thoughts because you get to really focus on what you are saying. Whenever you say an affirmation, you think it and see it in your mind. Creating short, powerful affirmations for your finances will turn your "I can't" into "I can," and help you get past your fears and translate your dreams into your reality.

Becoming very clear on your goals and your dreams will help you achieve them, but there's a downside. You see, as you start to get more specific about your dreams, your limiting beliefs will set in. Thoughts like "I will never be able to achieve this," or "Why am I wasting my time? This will never happen," or "Girl, who? You? Please," will start to run through your mind on repeat. You'll need to train your mind to get rid of those thoughts whenever they come up and replace them with empowering ones. This is where affirmations come in. Positive affirmations build the mental muscles that can be incredibly powerful for achieving goals and making your dreams a reality.

As you create affirmations to support bringing your dreams to reality, it's important to keep the following in mind:

- Your affirmations should be short and concise.
- They should be about your life and should be personal.
- They should be in the present tense.
- They should be positive.
- You should not compare yourself to anyone else when you create your affirmations.

Here are some examples of affirmations:

- Money is attracted to my bank account every single day.
- I am credit card debt free.
- I make good money decisions and invest wisely.

Once you create these affirmations, you want to refer to them often, so keep them visible and accessible. Save them as your phone screen saver, print them out and tape them to your bathroom mirror, put them on your fridge. The more you affirm, the more you believe you can, so the more you will!

Write down everything you want to accomplish in your life that's currently a big dream. Be very specific about what the dream is, down to the minute details. You should be able to tie each of these dreams to your financial goals.

    Next, using the example affirmations I provided in this section, write down your own list of affirmations that you can repeat to yourself daily. Feel free to include your affirmations as part of your daily meditations or prayers. *Think them, say them, believe them, receive them.*

CHAPTER 4

Shifting Your Circle of Influence

The people and things you surround yourself with (including what you read, what you listen to, and what you watch) have a strong impact on your finances, whether or not you choose to believe it. If you are continuously surrounded by people who think that they can never save, or that they can never pay off debt and are all about accepting what life gives them, then you are very likely to start thinking the same way because there's nothing motivating or empowering you to do better.

Shifting your circle of influence will not just help you get and stay motivated, but will also give you the opportunity to learn exactly how you can accomplish your goals from people who have already done what you are seeking to do. This, in turn, will change your mindset and your outlook on life, and positively impact your personal development and growth.

Use this section to take an assessment of your current circle of influence and reflect on your answers. For the yes or no answers, if the answer is mostly yes, select yes. If it's mostly no, select no:

Whom do you spend the most time with every day or every week? In person or using technology? (You can use initials or code names if you prefer)

	Yes	No
Do these relationships mostly encourage your goals and dreams?		
Do they motivate you to expand and accomplish more?		
Do they mostly hinder or derail your progress?		
Are any of these toxic relationships that you need to distance yourself from?		

What do you spend most of your free time doing?

	Yes	No
Are these activities mostly aligned with your long-term goals and values?		
Do they contribute to your personal growth and development?		
Are there hobbies or interests you want to explore that could also have a positive impact on your life?		

Based on your responses above, what shifts do you need to make to help you get on track with your life and financial goals?

CHAPTER **5**

Getting Your Financial Records in Order

It's so much easier to execute and be successful with a plan when you know where everything is and have easy access to all the information you need whenever you need it. At the very minimum, you'll be able to find things easily, and you'll be aware of any gaps you need to fill or issues you need to address around your financial records. To do this, you'll need to organize your bank accounts, your financial (and other related) records, and your insurance records. Let's go over the details.

Bank Accounts

Bank accounts are where you process the majority of your daily transactions, including your savings and investments, so it's important that you have the right accounts set up for your needs. Here are a few types of accounts you can have in place that can help you keep your money organized:

- A bill payment account for day-to-day spending, to pay your household bills, and for debt repayment
- An emergency savings account
- A short- to mid-term savings account, for goals like buying a house or car, or saving for a vacation
- Retirement investment accounts

- Nonretirement investment accounts – like savings for your child's college education and other long-term goals
- Separate business checking and savings accounts if you are a business owner

Personally, I have bill payment accounts, multiple short-term savings accounts (I like to keep my savings for different short-term goals separate), retirement savings accounts, investment accounts for my children's college education, and business savings and checking accounts.

The actual number of accounts you have really depends on you. It's all about making sure you are able to keep track of where your money is and what it's for. If you don't have much to keep track of, you can use fewer accounts and track those amounts separately. It really comes down to personal preference for how many accounts you hold and how you organize your money. The point is that you are aware of where your money is, where it should be going, and what you've already allocated it to.

Financial Records

We live in a day and age where security breaches and identity theft are becoming all too common, unfortunately, and so your financial records (whether physical or electronic) and the details of each record (account numbers, beneficiary information, specific contact information) should be stored in a safe place, like a home safe or an encrypted folder on your computer or in an encrypted cloud account. These records may include:

- Social Security cards
- Insurance policies
- Warranties
- Investment details
- Tax returns
- Loan documents
- Wills
- Nonfinancial records like diplomas and passports

The important thing is that you keep track of your records, know where everything is, and can access them when necessary. You may also want your partner, close relative, or lawyer to know where things are in the event that you need records but aren't available to get them yourself.

Insurance Records

The purpose of insurance is that it serves as your backup in the event of a serious situation. It means you won't have to derail your financial plans if something terrible happens. So, as part of this organization process, you'll want to review your insurance policies to make sure you have the right type of coverage for your individual life scenario and that you know where all the information is if you find you have to make a claim. At a minimum, your coverage should include:

- Auto insurance
- Health insurance
- Home or rental insurance
- Life insurance (if you have children or other people who depend on your income)
- Personal article insurance (if you own expensive jewelry, electronics, or other valuable items)
- Disability insurance

You may not necessarily have all these insurances at the moment, nor do you necessarily need all of them. The point here is to know what you do have and what you need, where your records are, and how you can make a claim if necessary. It also means you've updated your beneficiaries and figured out if there's any additional insurance you need.

Use the following checklist as a guide to get your financial records organized. If you'd like to document things like account numbers and passwords, organize this information into an app with encryption capabilities, a spreadsheet with a password, or a physical binder that you store securely.

My personal preference is to use a password-protected spreadsheet. If you chose this approach, you can customize the tabs to your preference, but here is how I organize the tabs:

- Bank accounts and investment accounts
- Bills, credit cards, and loans
- Tax information (state and federal)
- Warranty information

Financial Organization Checklist

☐	Make a list of all your bank accounts, including your savings and investment accounts. Open bank accounts you need. Close or repurpose bank accounts you don't use or need.
☐	Make a list of all your bills using a spreadsheet to organize them, or use an app and review your budget.
☐	Locate your tax returns and store them securely digitally or physically.
☐	Locate any warranty documentation, note their expiration dates, and store them securely (home, appliance, auto, repair, etc.).
☐	Locate any recurring statements you receive by physical mail or email. This includes statements for your investment, utility or mortgage payments, credit cards, student loans, and bank and insurance statements. Make a note of their physical or digital locations.
☐	Make sure you have the right type of insurance coverage for your life scenario as applicable: • Auto insurance • Health insurance • Home or rental insurance • Life insurance (if you have children or others who depend on your income) • Personal article insurance (if you own expensive jewelry, electronics or other items) • Disability insurance

Note: For all your financial records and bills, highlight the important information on them, like account numbers, contact phone numbers and addresses, interest rates, and so on. For digital documents, be sure to store them in password-protected or encrypted folders. For physical documents, it's a good idea to invest in a fireproof/waterproof home safe you keep in a secure location.

Depending on how much information you have, this exercise could take some time, but that's okay! Once you've gotten everything organized, you'll be so glad you did. It will give you a better sense of the big picture of your finances and help you make decisions later.

How Long Should I Keep My Records?

Honestly, this is one of the most common questions I'm asked when organization comes up. Knowing how long to keep your records will allow you to have everything you need when you need it, but also to keep your records as streamlined as possible. This way, you're not sifting through anything that's no longer needed, yet you don't get rid of anything you'll likely need in the future.

Here is a quick overview of how long you should keep your various financial records:

Active accounts and obligations: keep while active
- Insurance documents
- Contracts
- Retirement plan contributions
- Equity and stock records
- Brokerage statements
- Home improvement records
- Property tax records
- Ongoing debt repayments
- Records for items associated with active warranties
- Records for items that have not exceeded their return dates

Records to keep permanently
- Birth certificates or adoption paperwork
- Death certificates
- Marriage certificates
- Wills
- Records of mortgages you've paid off on housing, land, and other property
- IRA contribution statements for nondeductible contributions

Records to keep at least seven years
- Tax returns
- Tax-related records (e.g. alimony payments, charitable contributions)

Records to keep at least three years
- Canceled insurance policies
- Property sales (e.g. investments and real estate)
- Paid medical bills
- Capital gains and losses reports, other deductions for your tax returns

Records to keep at least one year

- Canceled checks
- Paycheck records
- Bill payment records
- Bank statements

▶ Thinking Ahead

Establish an estate plan: Consider what you would like to happen to your assets if you are no longer here, keeping your dependents in mind. One thing you can do is leverage estate planning as a means of passing down generational wealth. In addition to getting your financial documents in order, this would also include taking inventory of all your assets, establishing a will, forming a trust, and reviewing your health-care and life insurance options. There are several well-reviewed estate planning books online, and you can also consult with an estate planning professional to help you establish a plan.

CHAPTER **6**

Tracking
Your Spending

Tracking your spending can be an incredibly eye-opening exercise if you follow through. The whole point of tracking your money is to be more aware of your spending, help you identify your spending habits and money leaks, and help you identify areas for improvement.

Here are some costs you should pay attention to that are responsible for the biggest oversights when it comes to spending:

- **Food and groceries.** The cost of food continues to rise, and eating out on a consistent basis can eat up a huge chunk of your budget. And so being mindful of how much you are spending on food particularly can have a significant impact on your budget.

  So assess your fridge and your pantry to see what you have at home, and then create a food list before you go grocery shopping. When you shop, be sure to look out for your grocery store offers and sales. You can also consider meal planning to reduce how often you eat out or order in. Eating out comes with a higher price tag than cooking at home, and those food delivery fees can add up to a big deal over time!

- **Subscriptions.** In today's world, there's a subscription for pretty much everything, from entertainment streaming services to personal care products to pet products to meal services and more. Individually, many subscriptions are reasonably priced but when you have multiple subscriptions, the amount can add up. So if you're paying for subscriptions (or memberships) you hardly ever use, it's time to cancel them!

33

- **Brand-name products.** We all love a good brand name, but the truth is that there are several generic or store-brand alternatives that are just as good if not better than some of the brand-name items. It's worth exploring generic and store-brand alternatives to save some extra cash. For example, instead of the big brand names, I buy store-brand frozen vegetables. They taste the same, in my opinion! So save the cash where there's no difference, and that way you can splurge on the brand names you love.

- **Credit card interest.** If you can afford to pay more than the minimum on your credit cards each month but you don't, then that's a big money leak! This is because of the accruing compounding interest on your debt. So paying more than the minimum on your credit card reduces the compounding interest you'll accrue.

- **Not comparing prices.** Don't get comfortable with your cell phone, cable, or insurance bills – shop around for better deals! I have a reminder to do this once a year. It only takes a few minutes and if I find a better deal, I let my current provider know. Many times they will match the rates I find without me having to switch service providers. The savings is totally worth those few minutes of your time.

Other common spending oversights and money leaks include things like these:

- Purchasing more than you need because of discounts or promotions. Um, no, you don't need to spend an extra $50 to get free shipping when shipping costs $3.99!
- Recurring bank fees and charges. It's worth shopping around to find the free checking and savings accounts.
- Paying for services you can easily do yourself. Pay to get your nails done if that brings you joy but you can watch a YouTube video on how to hang up a painting and save yourself the handyman fee!

Tracking your spending ensures that you are aware of where your money is going. By doing this, you can avoid wasting money and put the money you don't spend toward the things that bring you joy or toward paying down debt, saving, or investing!

To start tracking your spending, at least for the first couple of weeks, I highly recommend a pen and notebook (a spending journal) that you carry around with you. Later you can transition over to an app or even a simple spreadsheet.

Why? There's just something about putting pen to paper when you first start this exercise and seeing things laid out in your own handwriting that helps with perspective. Psychology, magic – call it what you will, it works!

To be successful in tracking your spending, you need to commit to writing down every single transaction you make every single day for those first two weeks – from a pack of gum to coffee to lunch, whether you used your debit card, spent cash, or used your credit card. Every single transaction should go into your spending journal. You can either write down your transactions as they happen or collect all your receipts and document your transactions at the end of each day.

Set a daily reminder to spend five minutes going over your spending for each day. (If you don't spend anything on a particular day, celebrate with a happy dance!) Then set a weekly reminder for 15–30 minutes to review things in more detail at the end of each week.

Here's a 14-day spending journal you can use. Alternatively, you can get a dedicated notebook for this or use the notes app on your smartphone.

14-Day Spending Journal Worksheet
Add a bookmark to this section so you can easily come back to it while you track your spending over the two-week period.

Day 1

Category	Description	What you spent	What it was for	How you felt

Day 2

Category	Description	What you spent	What it was for	How you felt

Day 3

Category	Description	What you spent	What it was for	How you felt

Day 4

Category	Description	What you spent	What it was for	How you felt

Day 5

Category	Description	What you spent	What it was for	How you felt

Day 6

Category	Description	What you spent	What it was for	How you felt

Day 7

Category	Description	What you spent	What it was for	How you felt

Day 8

Category	Description	What you spent	What it was for	How you felt

Day 9

Category	Description	What you spent	What it was for	How you felt

Day 10

Category	Description	What you spent	What it was for	How you felt

Day 11

Category	Description	What you spent	What it was for	How you felt

Day 12

Category	Description	What you spent	What it was for	How you felt

Day 13

Category	Description	What you spent	What it was for	How you felt

Day 14

Category	Description	What you spent	What it was for	How you felt

You can also take things a step further by pulling out the last three months of your credit card and bank statements to look at how you've spent money historically. This can help you begin to piece together your spending patterns and provide a baseline for your analysis: Are there areas where you consistently overspend or make impulse purchases? Are there any bills or services you are paying too much for or don't need altogether?

As part of this analysis, mark up your highest spending categories to determine where you've spent the most and where you see opportunities to scale back. Certain apps will do this for you automatically, but you can also use a highlighter in your journal to start out. Keep all of these insights in mind as you track your spending going forward.

Based on this review of your statements, use the next chart to break your spending out into categories to see what you spent where (what percentage of your total monthly spending is each category?), and determine where you can cut back and by how much.

For example, you may realize that your food category makes up 10% of your total monthly spending and within that category, half of that money is spent on eating out. This could be an opportunity for you to cut back by making more meals at home and setting a fixed budget for eating out.

Category	% of overall spending	Opportunities to cut back/ Action steps

Category	% of overall spending	Opportunities to cut back/ Action steps

As you track, you'll start to find that you are more aware of your spending habits, and you will even start to make better decisions around your money. That's because now you're actively thinking things through as opposed to spending money without giving it much thought. You may also find that you are spending less, which is the perfect opportunity to use those freed-up funds toward your debt repayment or savings.

CHAPTER **7**

Breaking Up with Your Bad Money Habits

Often, we start up a habit slowly, like overspending, without even realizing it's happening. Then several months pass and you've gone way over budget. Now you try to stop the spending, but it's become a part of your routine – breaking it becomes a serious challenge. And this is the big problem – habits are just incredibly hard to break.

Some of the most common bad money habits include:

- Overspending
- Not creating a monthly budget
- Paying your bills late
- Carrying a credit card balance that you don't pay in full each month, even when you have the cash to do so
- Using your emergency fund for things that are not emergencies (ahem, coffee and manicures – not emergencies)
- Not saving because you think you don't earn enough
- Not investing because you think you are too young, too old, it's too complicated, or you'll just figure it out later
- Paying for subscription services that you never use

Do any of the above sound familiar? Can you relate to scenarios where you find yourself committing these bad habit offenses time and time again?

If you are trying to break a bad money habit or two, you'll need to:

1. First, identify each of your bad money habits, including where you find yourself doing them and the feelings that trigger them.
2. Next, plan out in advance what actions you can take to replace the habit or actions that trigger the habit.

That said, use the next worksheet for the following exercise to help you curb any bad money habits you want to get rid of!

1. Make a list of every single bad money habit you have that comes to mind, organized by level of severity or impact on your finances. Not sure what they are? Go over your credit card and bank statements and review your spending.
2. For each habit, write down the triggers (including time and place) or the behaviors that cause you to engage in this habit. If you're not sure, monitor yourself – when you catch yourself thinking about or doing that habit, take note of how you're feeling and what led you there.
3. Assess whether your habits and triggers are associated with any money myths you might believe. Make a note of what the myth is and then write down why that myth is a lie! For example:
   • Money myth #1: Money is the root of all evil.
   • Money myth #2: You need a lot of money to invest.
   • Money myth #3: Personal finance is hard, so leave it to the professionals.
   • Money myth #4: It's not polite to talk about money.
   • Money myth #5: Getting your finances in order is punishment.
4. Next, come up with an alternative action that you can take when this trigger happens. Perhaps you change your route to work, avoid certain stores, keep cash at home – whatever it is, try to do this consistently to help yourself, rather than leaving it up to willpower.
5. Finally, determine a reward you can give yourself if you are able to stay consistent with breaking your habit. For example, if you stay away from the coffee shop for a month, maybe treat yourself to a cup. Or maybe buy yourself a fancy coffee machine for home (that you've planned for in your budget).

#	Bad money habits to break	Habit trigger	Associated money myth	Alternative action to take	Reward
1					
2					
3					
4					
5					
6					
7					
8					

CHAPTER **8**

Your Net Worth

Tracking your net worth will show you what kind of progress you're making and help you see that your small changes impact the big picture. (I promise, they really do!) **Your net worth shows you where you stand financially and helps you create a plan of attack to get your numbers up.**

However, calculating and tracking net worth can be a touchy subject. While some people love doing it, others might hate facing the reality of what their net worth might be at the current moment. Notice my emphasis on "current moment" here. Remember, where you are right now is only temporary, and you are now taking the steps to make real progress on improving things. After all, that's why you're taking the action steps in this workbook, right?

So, let's work those numbers out.

How to Calculate Your Net Worth

Your net worth is calculated by subtracting your liabilities from your assets.

Net worth = Assets (what you own) − Liabilities (what you owe)

Yup, that's it. It's basically taking the value of all the things you owe (mortgages, credit card debt, student loans, car loans, etc.) from the value of all the things you own (real estate, vehicles, cash, investments, jewelry, etc.).

So let's say, for example, you own your own home and have a bit of retirement savings, but also have a mortgage, student loans, and credit card debt. Your net worth calculation would be the total value of your home and retirement accounts minus the value of your mortgage, student loans, and credit card debt.

Your assets (what you own), for example:
• The value of your house and any other real estate you might own • The sum of your retirement savings • The sum in your bank accounts
MINUS (–)
Your liabilities (what you owe), for example:
• The balance on your mortgage • The balance on your student loans • Your total credit card debt
EQUALS (=)
Your net worth (as of the specified date)

Now it's your turn. Let's work on calculating your net worth. On the worksheet:

1. Make a list of all your assets – the things you own.
2. Make a list of all your liabilities – what you owe.
3. Subtract your liabilities from your assets to get your net worth.
4. Make note of today's date and then set a reminder to repeat this exercise every quarter so you can track the progress you make as you take action toward your financial goals.

Date: _____

Assets*		Liabilities	
Cash savings		Mortgage	
Retirement accounts		Student loans	
Non-retirement investment accounts		Car note	
Primary residence		Credit cards	
_____		_____	
_____		_____	
_____		_____	
_____		_____	
_____		_____	
_____		_____	
Total Assets		**Total Liabilities**	

Under assets, include valuables that have monetary value (e.g. you can sell them for cash).

My Net Worth (Assets – Liabilities): _____

If your net worth is negative, don't panic! Many people start out with a negative net worth. If this is you, it's okay. A negative net worth usually occurs when you haven't earned enough or invested enough of your income to offset your debt. For example, it's not uncommon for younger people who have student loans to have a negative net worth, because they typically haven't earned much at the beginning of their career.

Another reason for a negative net worth could be overspending and having large amounts of credit card debt without many assets to offset them. Given time and the continuous practice of good financial habits, this can change.

How to Increase Your Net Worth

Every time you make a payment toward debt, or you put money in your savings account, you are increasing your net worth.

Even if it still remains negative, when you make a debt payment you are reducing the total amount of debt you carry, which in turn increases your net worth and will gradually move you out of the negative (the red) and into the positive (the black).

Here are some impactful moves you can take to increase your net worth:

- Increase the amount you pay toward your debts each month (paying more than the minimum).
- Acquire more long-term investments to increase your assets. (Investing in your retirement plan is a great example of this.) Additionally, you can also invest outside of retirement in things like stocks, bonds, or real estate that have the potential for growth.
- Find ways to reduce your expenses and increase your income so you can put more money toward paying down debt and saving or investing more.
- Review your financial goals and progress on a regular basis, so you can adjust as needed to stay on track toward increasing your net worth.

Ultimately, increasing your net worth is just a matter of time and focused effort. You've got this!

CHAPTER **9**

Your Core Values

Your core values are the things in life that are most important to you.** In other words, these are the things you hold onto above all else. To be able to live the life of your dreams, you need to know what's most important to you in your life and prioritize these things accordingly. When your goals are structured around the things that really matter to you, you are more compelled to actually do what it takes to achieve them.

Defining your core values is a personal thing. What's most important to me might be completely different from what's most important to you, so when you work on defining your values, don't worry about what other people are doing. Instead, focus on what you really want and, most importantly, what will make you happy.

Typically, people's core values revolve around experiences, financial security, giving back, and their loved ones. For instance, if one of your dreams is to become a world traveler, exploring new cultures and different destinations, then one of your core values is *experience*.

If you want to build long-term wealth for you and your family so you can afford the nicer things in life and have peace of mind about money, then one of your core values is *financial security*.

If you want to build a school for less privileged children or give back to single mothers in need, then a core value of yours is *giving back*.

Not sure how to identify your core values? One exercise I love to do with people that really gets them thinking is what I call the Million-Dollar Game. Here's how it works.

All you need is a timer, a piece of paper, and a pen. In 10 minutes, I want you to write down what you'd do if I gave you $1 million, tax free with no strings attached. Once you're finished, take a look at the list – what did you choose to spend money on? Was it a luxury life-style? An experience? Charity? Or did you invest or save it? This exer-cise usually gets things flowing when it comes to outlining what really matters to you.

Once you've gone through the exercise of identifying your core val-ues, you then want to prioritize them in the order in which you'd like to achieve them. Once you've done that, you'll have a solid foundation on which to build your financial goals.

Let's play the Million-Dollar Game:

1. Set your timer for 10 minutes and write down what you'd do if I gave you $1 million with no strings attached. You can make a list, draw, or scribble – there is no order to how it should be done. There are no rules.
2. As you do the exercise, tap into your daydreams about how you imagine your life would be if money was no object, not worrying about what other people are thinking or doing.
3. Once the timer is up, organize your notes into a list in order of prior-ity and tie each priority to a value: experiences, loved ones, financial security, giving back, and so on.
4. Finally, make a note of why each value is important to you.

Set your timer for 10 minutes and lay out your million-dollar plan. Make a list, draw, or scribble. Don't worry about the order right now.

Now organize your plan into a list in order of priority and tie each priority to a value that's important to you (experiences, loved ones, financial security, giving back, etc.).

	Plan	Value	Why this is important to me
1			
2			
3			
4			
5			
6			
7			
8			
9			
10			

Now that you know what your core values are, reference them often. Keep in mind that it's okay for them to change or shift in priority as you navigate through life.

CHAPTER **10**

Your Financial (and Life) Goals

Now that you know what you value and where you really want to be in life, let's talk about goals – specifically, your financial goals. **Your financial goals are essentially the objectives you want to achieve with money based on the type of life you want to live or the future financial needs you will have.**

Having solid financial goals in place gives you something specific to work toward, which in turn makes you more likely to achieve your objectives. In other words, having financial goals will set you on the path toward your financial success. It's one of the things that will help you tell your money where it needs to go.

Personally, having clear financial goals has been a major contributor to the success I've had with my finances. My goals have kept me focused and grounded even when I've veered off course. Having those goals reminds me of the big picture of what I want to accomplish with my money. That way I'm able to get myself back on track.

Think about anything you've ever wanted to accomplish in your life that you committed to working on. It was probably tied to a goal linked to a desired result or end state that you wanted to have. The same applies to your financial goals. Having clear goals can keep you on track when it comes to paying off debt, managing your spending, saving money, and investing.

53

As you start to think of your financial goals, you should use your core values as a baseline. You also want to ensure the goals you create are specific and measurable, and based on the values and priorities you set in the last section. It also often helps to break your goals down into short-, mid-, and long-term ones.

Your Short-Term Goals

Short-term goals are the ones you want to accomplish within the next five years. So, for example, if debt freedom is at the top of your core values list and you want to pay off all your credit card debt within five years, then you would add this to your list of short-term goals.

To make it specific and measurable, you'll need to determine how much you owe in total and figure out how much you can afford to pay down each month in order for you to become debt free by a certain date.

Based on your specific situation, your goal might look something like this: "Pay $500 a month toward my credit card debt in order to become debt free in the next 36 months."

Your Mid-Term Goals

Mid-term goals would be the goals you want to accomplish in the next 5–10 years. So if homeownership is on your core values list, then saving up money for a down payment on a house might be at the top of your mid-term goal list.

To make it specific, add details of how much you will save and for how long. It might look something like this: "Save $500 a month for the next 72 months for a $36,000 (10%) down payment on our first home."

Your Long-Term Goals

Long-term goals are the ones you want to accomplish 10–15 (or more) years from now. For instance, if financial security is top on your core values list, then an example of a long-term financial goal might be to start saving for your retirement.

Your goal might be something like this: "Max out my annual 401(k) and target-date retirement fund contributions each year in order to amass $1,000,000 to retire comfortably in 30 years."

Taking your short-, mid-, and long-term goals into account, your financial goal list and priorities might look something like this:

My Financial Goals

- *Priority 1:* Become debt free. Pay $500 a month toward my credit card debt in order to become debt free in the next 36 months (short-term goal).
- *Priority 2:* Purchase our first home. Save $500 a month for the next 72 months for a $36,000 (10%) down payment on our first home (mid-term goal).
- *Priority 3:* Retire in 30 years. Max out my annual 401(k) and target-date retirement fund contributions each year in order to amass $1,000,000 to retire comfortably (long-term goal).

Once you've outlined your goals, you can then build them into your budget and start tracking your progress on a monthly, quarterly, and annual basis. The goals would also directly tie into improving your net worth.

Work on laying out your financial goals:

1. Go over your core values. What are the things that are most important to you in your life?
2. What would you like to achieve in the next 5, 10, and 15-plus years? Stick to three to five major financial goals.
3. Prioritize your goals out into short-term (less than 5 years), mid-term (5–10 years), and long-term (10-plus years) goals.
4. Determine the dollar amount for each of your goals and write them out specifically. You'll then need to build line items in your budget to save and invest toward each goal each time you get paid. (We discuss budgeting in the next section.)
5. As your finances change, reevaluate your goals. If you get a raise or find a better-paying job, you might be able to increase your contributions to each goal or add new ones. So set a reminder in your phone to check in every quarter.

	Financial goal	Dollar amount ($)	Timeline (short-term, mid-term, long-term)
1			
2			
3			
4			
5			

CHAPTER **11**

Your Budget

Having a budget of some form is truly important for your financial success. **Your budget tells your money what to do – not the other way around.** When you manage your money with a budget, every cent is accounted for, and you have full control over how much you spend and how much you save. You see, you are the boss of your money, and you work way too hard for it to let it just slip through your fingers.

I personally prefer the word *plan* to the word *budget* because it doesn't sound so constraining. So, if it helps, instead of your calling your outline for where your money goes a boring old budget, call it something you like that you'd be happy to do – or at the very least happy about your budget-naming skills – for instance, My Prosperity Plan or My Amazing Life Plan.

Basically, call it something you like that will motivate the heck out of you every time you think about it.

Give it a try!

Name your budget something fun:

_____

It also helps when you look at your money objectively for what it really is – a tool to help you get the things you truly desire in life. That being said, here are a few tips to be successful with budgeting:

• **Create a budget in advance of each month.** Creating a budget a few days in advance of each month means that once the month starts, you have a plan, and you aren't scrambling trying to figure out what to do. You'll find a budget template you can get started with in this section. To download printable pdf and Excel versions of it to use each month, visit http://clevergirlfinance.com/my-wealth-plan.

- **Don't assume every month will be the same.** Every single month should be planned separately. No two months will be exactly the same financially, so you want to prepare in advance for things like one-off bills and one-time expenses, travel plans, or events you have to attend.
- **Base your budget on your projected income for that month.** If you get paid once a month, twice a month, or every two weeks, base your budget on that projected income so you know exactly how much you have to budget. Keep in mind that if you get paid every two weeks, there will be months where you get three paychecks.
- **Pay your expenses before splurging.** This means paying for your essentials, debts, and goals (savings and investments) first before you do any splurging or miscellaneous spending. The last thing you want is to find that you have overspent on what isn't necessary and don't have a way to pay your bills.
- **Track your transactions.** Tracking your transactions allows you to make sure you stay within your budget and keeps you conscious of your spending habits. You can track your transactions in a spending journal, a spreadsheet, or with an automated app or online tool.
- **Practice makes perfect.** Think of budgeting like riding a bike. You are going to fall off a few times, maybe even bruise your knee, but to master riding that bike, you'll need to get up each time and keep going. The same thing applies to your budget. It might not be perfect every month, but if you keep working at it, you can get pretty close and it will make all the difference when it comes to managing your money!

Your Budget Categories

If you don't have budget categories in place yet, you can break down your monthly budget into the following four categories:

1. **Money for your future self and your emergency fund.** Before you pay any bills or do any shopping, a portion of your earnings should be diverted into your retirement account for your future self and your emergency savings accounts for a rainy day. No ifs, no maybes. Just do it.

   Having an emergency fund will provide you with a buffer in the event of unforeseen problems. You can rely on your emergency savings instead of a credit card or other debt to pay off something that comes up unexpectedly.

   Included in this category (or as a subcategory) should be money to pay off any debt you have. It's essential that you pay off your debt as soon as you can so you can shift your focus to building long-term wealth.

2. **Your essentials.** Next would be your essentials and needs – the things you need to live your life. This does not include money for shopping or getting your nails done; those are not essentials (neither are they emergencies). This is for things like your housing costs (mortgage or rent), transportation, and food.
3. **Your other financial and life goals.** This would include money you are saving outside of your retirement account – your mid-term and long-term savings and investments, for instance, or saving for a home purchase or your kids' college.
4. **Everything else.** This is where your splurge money would fall – money you would spend shopping or saving for a wish list item, eating out, traveling, entertaining yourself, and whatever else it is that you would typically do to enjoy your life.

If You Have Children

When creating your budget, be sure to include not only your own expenses but also those of your children. School activities, clothes, trips, and weekend activities are all things that should be budgeted. This way, you know exactly how to plan out your income each month.

You also want to ensure that your emergency fund covers your children. Your goal for your emergency fund should be to have three to six months of your basic living expenses put away in the event of a true emergency, such as a job loss. It's also a good idea to include your children's basic expenses as part of your emergency account.

Finally, be sure to include a line item in your budget for saving for your child's future.

If You Have Debt

If you have debt (credit cards, student loans, auto loans, or personal loans), you should plan to pay as much as you can toward your debt each month. To do this, you'll have to lower the amounts you contribute to your different budget categories and reallocate your funds to paying off your debt as quickly as you can.

If You Need to Catch Up on Your Retirement Savings

Again, you'd need to make adjustments to your budget categories to accommodate extra savings toward your retirement by shifting things around or cutting back in some areas altogether. For instance, you could cut back on the "everything else" category and instead apply those funds to your retirement accounts.

Budgeting Styles

One of the reasons so many people shy away from budgeting is that it can seem tedious, annoying, and even difficult. As a result, they struggle with successfully creating and sticking to their budget. However, there are a variety of ways to budget, and your success with budgeting can be greatly improved by changing your budgeting style.

The style you choose is entirely up to you. The most important part is picking one that works for your life and one that you (can grow to) like, even if you currently hate budgeting. In fact, you can just try one that sounds like it might work for you. If it doesn't, you can switch styles until you find your groove.

The point is that you need to figure out a way to budget that works with your personality and personal style. Because budgeting is important, there really should be no excuse for not doing it. Here are four budgeting styles you can try. Once you determine what style best works for you, you can use it to structure your budget.

The Percentage Breakdown

This popular budgeting style is probably the most common one. In this method, you break your income into percentages and then plan out your spending and savings accordingly. The most popular percentage breakdown is the **50-30-20 budgeting method**:

- Your needs/essentials (shelter, food, transportation, insurance) = 50%
- Your wants/nonessentials (travel, entertainment, dining out, hobbies) = 30%
- Money for the future (retirement savings, kids, college fund), your emergency fund, debt repayment beyond the minimum required payments, and other long-term goals = 20%

Keep in mind that these percentages are not set in stone. For instance, you can choose to spend less on your needs/essentials and wants/nonessentials and put more to savings or debt. Some other common percentage breakdowns include:

- **80-20:** 20% of your income is allocated toward savings and debt, while the remaining 80% covers both your essential and nonessential expenses.

- **70-20-10:** 70% of your income is allocated toward your essential and nonessential expenses, 20% of your income is set aside for savings, and the remaining 10% is used to pay down debt.
- **60-30-10:** 60% of your income goes toward savings, debt payoff, and investments, 30% is budgeted for your essential expenses, and 10% is for nonessentials.
- **30-30-30-10:** 30% of your income goes toward your housing costs, 30% goes toward your savings goals, 30% pays for your essential expenses including debt, and the final 10% is for nonessentials.

As you review your needs/essentials, wants/nonessentials, and your savings and debt repayment goals, you may decide to select a 35-30-35 breakdown, a 35-35-40 breakdown, or even a 25-25-50 breakdown. Ultimately, the goal is to set percentage breakdowns that make sense for you.

Who This Budgeting Style Is Good For

If your income and expenses are fixed, for the most part, and you want a clear-cut approach to splitting up your finances, this approach would work well for you. To be successful with it, you want to make sure that you look closely at your breakdown and adjust things as necessary based on your financial situation. Ultimately, the goal with your percentages should be to help you improve your financial situation, whether that is paying off debt or saving more.

The Envelope or Cash System

This works by subtracting your expenses from your income and then putting each expense amount into its own envelope. This would include things like bills you need to pay and your day-to-day spending.

You can keep the money for your big bills in virtual envelopes that you track through a spreadsheet or app and then put actual cash for your smaller expenses or day-to-day transactions in actual physical envelopes.

Once the envelope for a particular expense is depleted, you can no longer spend money in that category unless it is an emergency. If you don't spend all the money in a particular expense envelope, you can repurpose the funds toward something else like savings or debt.

Who This Budgeting Style Is Good For

If you struggle with sticking to a budget or with overspending, then this budget approach could work well for you. That's because it's harder to spend cash than it is to spend money on a debit or credit card – you actually see the dollar bills leaving your envelopes!

With this method, you are clear about what money is meant for what part of your budget. If you do choose this method, be mindful of where you keep your envelopes. Since you'll be operating partially or wholly in cash, you want to be sure you don't lose anything!

Reverse Budgeting

Reverse budgeting is a method where you focus on a single goal, such as paying off a certain amount of debt or saving a certain amount of money each month in addition to paying your bills. And then, as long as you meet your monthly goal and pay your bills without exceeding your income, you can do what you like with the money you have left over.

Who This Budgeting Style Is Good For

This approach could work for you if your finances are simple, you have fixed bills, and you're following a savings or debt repayment strategy that fits into your current income.

You'd still want to make sure you are aware of and are tracking all your bills, debt payments, and savings amounts so you can monitor your payments and track your progress toward accomplishing your goals.

Using Apps

Apps make it really simple to budget, especially if you can connect your bank accounts to them. They eliminate the manual aspect of tracking your transactions – for the most part, all you need to do is check in frequently to ensure your transactions are tracked the right way and set up alerts to keep you on top of your budget.

You can set up your budget to be reflective of any of the above budgeting methods.

Who This Budgeting Style Is Good For

Budgeting with an app basically automates your tracking, which can make things really simple. At the same time, it can detach you from closely monitoring your finances if you don't make a conscious effort to do so. You want to make sure that if you are using an app, you are checking in on your budget frequently and reviewing your category breakdowns to ensure your app is accurately matching your transactions to the right budget categories.

■ ■ ■

If you are undecided about which approach to use, test each out for a month to determine what works best for you based on which one is easiest to use and fits into your money management style. You might also choose to use a hybrid or combination of these different styles.

Ultimately, when it comes to budgeting, whatever is easiest is best. The easier or more manageable you make it, the more likely you are to do it – and that's what truly matters here.

Create Your Monthly Budget and Emergency Savings Plan

Based on your budgeting style of choice, leverage the budgeting worksheet and emergency savings worksheet to create a brand-new budget or adjust your existing one. Feel free to modify it to best suit your needs. Here are some key tips:

- Add up all your sources of regular income.
- Next, list all of your expenses for each month. This will include your fixed costs like rent/mortgage, utilities, and insurance, as well as your variable costs like groceries, entertainment, transportation, and so on. Don't forget to include your savings (paying yourself first and emergency savings) and debt repayments as expenses.
- If you aren't sure what all of your expenses are, go over the last three months of your bank and credit card statements to see what you pay for on a recurring basis.
- In addition, review the expenses you know you have coming up in the month and include those items in your budget as well.
- Add up the numbers to determine your income versus your expenses.
- If your expenses exceed your income, brainstorm where you can cut back and/or how you can earn more.
- If your income covers your expenses, challenge yourself to widen the gap between your income and your expenses. Again, brainstorm where you can cut back and/or how you can earn more.

Simple Monthly Budget

Monthly budget for: _____

Income	Details (Earned from etc)	Amount	Notes
Paycheck Income			
Other Income _____			
Total Income		$	

Category	Details (Account names, etc)	Budgeted Amount	Actual Spent	Difference (– under / + over)	Notes
Long term / Emergency Savings					
Retirement					
Emergency Fund					
Essentials / Needs					
Mortgage / Rent					
Home Insurance					
Auto Insurance					
Electricity					
Water					
Gas					
Phone					
Groceries					
_____					
_____					
_____					

Category	Details (Account names, etc)	Budgeted Amount	Actual Spent	Difference (– under / + over)	Notes
Debt Payoff					
_____					
_____					
_____					
_____					
_____					
_____					
Other Savings & Investments					
College Savings					
_____					
_____					
_____					
Everything Else					
Eating Out					
Travel					
Shopping					
_____					
_____					
_____					
	Total Expenses	$	$	$	
	Total Income - Actual Spent	$	$	$	

If you haven't already settled on a budgeting style, use the following steps to determine which one could work best for you:

1. Pick a style discussed in this section to test out for a month.
2. Establish your budget based on the style you decide on and then set reminders to actively track your budget at least once a week.
3. As you make progress throughout the month, take note of what is working and what isn't when it comes to that particular style.
4. If you find that it doesn't work for you, test out a new style the following month, using the steps above.

Emergency Savings Worksheet

This worksheet will help you determine exactly how much you need to put away in emergency savings. List your monthly costs for each of your essentials. Leave out the "nice to have" items – these are the items that are not essential to you getting by each month.

Essential expenses	Monthly cost
Mortgage/Rent	
Food	
Transportation costs	
Core utilities	
Total cost of essentials	$

3-month emergency savings estimate *Total cost of monthly essentials × 3*	$
6-month emergency savings estimate *Total cost of monthly essentials × 6*	$
12-month emergency savings estimate *Total cost of monthly essentials × 12*	$

Based on the amount you need for your emergency fund, determine how much you can put aside each time you get paid toward this goal and build it into your budget.

CHAPTER **12**

Paying Down Your Debt (Credit Cards, Student Loans, etc.)

While it's easy to get overwhelmed if you have a ton of debt to pay, the good news is that with changed spending habits and reprior-itizing your finances, you can start paying off your debt and have peace of mind.

Below are some key actions that will assist you on your journey to becoming debt free:

- **Get radical about your debt.** Make a mental commitment to getting rid of your debt. You want to get it out of your life as soon as you can.
- **Write it all down.** Visual representation of your debt is the most important step. This will give you an overview of all your debt in one place. Gather all your credit card statements, overdrafts, and loan statements and write down the amount you owe for each one of these items, along with their associated interest rate.

  At this point, it's also important to differentiate between good debt and bad. An example of good debt is a mortgage: a home is an asset that could potentially appreciate in value over the long term, despite the ups and downs of the real estate market. At the very least, if you pay off your mortgage, you'll end up owning your home outright.

  An example of bad debt is your credit card: this is a liability. You've spent the money – it's gone – and you are left paying high interest on an item that's probably not doing anything for you or that you may not even remember.

Keep in mind, though, that debt is still debt. Good and bad debts are still liabilities you'll eventually have to pay. You are just prioritizing by moving the good debt to the bottom of your payoff list and putting the bad debt at the top.

- **Put your list where you can see it every day.** There's nothing like a jolt back to reality when you're getting ready to go out wearing the latest designer shoes and you have your debt staring right in your face on your bathroom mirror. Having your debt listed in a place where you see it every day will keep your mind on track.
- **Cut up those credit cards.** So now you have your list written and posted in a place you'll see it all the time. Why are those credit cards still in your wallet? You don't need them. If you can't bear cutting them up, put them in a plastic bag, fill it up with water, and put that bag in the freezer until you've paid each one of them off, never to be used again.
- **Create a debt repayment strategy.** Having a debt repayment strategy in place that you build into your budget will guide you in paying off your debt as quickly as possible while minimizing the amount of interest you pay over the life of that debt. The debt snowball or debt avalanche are excellent strategies to use. You can leverage the debt prioritization worksheet at the end of this section to help you lay out your plans depending on which repayment method you choose.
- **Create an emergency fund.** As you pay off your debt, you should also start building a small emergency fund. Save $50–$100 from each paycheck until you get to $1000, so that if something comes up, instead of turning to a credit card and adding to your existing debt load, you can turn to your savings, and deal with your emergency.

When it comes to paying off your debt, you need to have a strategy in place that will help you pay it off as quickly as possible. The two most popular strategies are the debt snowball method and the debt avalanche method. Here's how you can use them to your advantage.

The Debt Snowball Method

The debt snowball method is a debt payoff strategy where you pay off multiple credit card balances by starting with the smallest balances first, regardless of interest rate. You pay as much as you can toward that small balance while paying the minimum payment on your larger debts.

Once that first small balance is gone, you take that payment and combine it with the minimum payment on the next smallest balance and you keep going that way until you are making a giant snowball payment against your largest debt, and that debt eventually gets paid off.

Here's a simple example. Let's say you have four debts of $6000, $3000, $2000, and $500 for a total of $11,500. With the debt snowball method, your plan would be to pay off the smallest debt first, regardless of the interest rate, so you would order them accordingly:

| Debt 1: $500 ($50 minimum payment) |
| Debt 2: $2000 ($65 minimum payment) |
| Debt 3: $3000 ($70 minimum payment) |
| Debt 4: $6000 ($165 minimum payment) |

Now, you determine that you can afford to pay $800 toward your total debt each month, based on your budget. In month one, you would start by paying the minimum payments on Debts 2–4. Then the rest of your debt payoff funds would go toward paying down Debt 1. So you would pay the minimum payment plus an additional $450.

By month two, you would have paid off Debt 1. You will then continue paying the minimum payments to Debts 3 and 4. The rest of your funds will now go toward paying down Debt 2. You would continue to follow this process until you've paid off Debt 4 in full.

	Payoff total	Minimum amount due	Amount toward next debt	Amount owed after this month			
				Debt 1	Debt 2	Debt 3	Debt 4
Month 1	800	350	450	$500	$2000	$3000	$6000
Month 2	800	350	450	$0	$1935	$2930	$5835
Month 3	800	300	500	$0	$1370	$2860	$5670
Month 4	800	300	500	$0	$805	$2790	$5505
Month 5	800	300	500	$0	$240	$2720	$5340
Month 6	800	300	500	$0	$0	$2325	$5175
Month 7	800	235	565	$0	$0	$1690	$5010
Month 8	800	235	565	$0	$0	$1055	$4845
Month 9	800	235	565	$0	$0	$420	$4680

	Payoff total	Minimum amount due	Amount toward next debt	Amount owed after this month			
				Debt 1	Debt 2	Debt 3	Debt 4
Month 10	800	235	565	$0	$0	$0	$4300
Month 11	800	235	565	$0	$0	$0	$3500
Month 12	800	165	635	$0	$0	$0	$2700
Month 13	800	165	635	$0	$0	$0	$1900
Month 14	800	165	635	$0	$0	$0	$1100
Month 15	800	165	635	$0	$0	$0	$300
Month 16	800	165	635	$0	$0	$0	$0

Note: This is a simplified example and does not account for reduced minimum payments as debts are paid down.

It works because as human beings, many of us thrive on and get motivated by quick wins. So paying off the smallest balances first, regardless of interest rate, will help you make quick progress and will motivate you to attack the rest of your debt.

The Debt Avalanche Method

The debt avalanche method is where you pay off your debt with the highest interest rate first, regardless of the size of the balance. The process then continues from there.

This plan will save you money in the long run as compared with the debt snowball method. That's because you pay off your high-interest debts first, reducing the amount of interest you pay overall. The drawback is that your first win might take some time.

For example, let's say you have four debts totaling $28,500, broken down as follows:

$10,000 at 15% interest
$9500 at 7% interest
$7000 at 12% interest
$2000 at 5% interest

With the avalanche method, your plan would be to pay off the debt with the highest interest rate first, so you would order them accordingly:

| Debt 1: $10,000 at 15% interest ($250 minimum payment) |
| Debt 2: $7000 at 12% interest ($195 minimum payment) |
| Debt 3: $9500 at 7% interest ($180 minimum payment) |
| Debt 4: $2000 at 5% interest ($50 minimum payment) |

You've determined that you can pay $1000 toward your debt each month, so, similar to the snowball method, you would pay the minimum payments on Debts 2–4, then you would pay the minimum payment plus whatever is left over (in this case, $325) toward Debt 1. Your repayment would go as follows:

	Payoff total	Minimum amount due	Amount toward next debt	Amount owed after this month			
				Debt 1	Debt 2	Debt 3	Debt 4
Month 1	1000	675	325	$10,000	$7000	$9500	$2000
Month 2	1000	675	325	$9550	$6875	$9375	$1958
Month 3	1000	675	325	$9094	$6749	$9250	$1916
Month 4	1000	675	325	$8633	$6621	$9124	$1874
Month 5	1000	675	325	$8166	$6492	$8997	$1832
Month 6	1000	675	325	$7693	$6362	$8870	$1790
Month 7	1000	675	325	$7214	$6231	$8742	$1747
Month 8	1000	675	325	$6729	$6098	$8613	$1705
Month 9	1000	675	325	$6239	$5964	$8483	$1662
Month 10	1000	675	325	$5741	$5829	$8352	$1619
Month 11	1000	675	325	$5238	$5692	$8221	$1575
Month 12	1000	675	325	$4729	$5554	$8089	$1532
Month 13	1000	675	325	$4213	$5415	$7956	$1488
Month 14	1000	675	325	$3690	$5274	$7823	$1445
Month 15	1000	675	325	$3162	$5132	$7688	$1401
Month 16	1000	675	325	$2626	$4988	$7553	$1356
Month 17	1000	675	325	$2084	$4843	$7417	$1312
Month 18	1000	675	325	$1535	$4696	$7280	$1268

	Payoff total	Minimum amount due	Amount toward next debt	Amount owed after this month			
				Debt 1	Debt 2	Debt 3	Debt 4
Month 19	1000	425	575	$979	$4548	$7143	$1223
Month 20	1000	425	575	$416	$4399	$7004	$1178
Month 21	1000	425	575	$0	$4094	$6865	$1133
Month 22	1000	425	575	$0	$3365	$6725	$1088
Month 23	1000	425	575	$0	$2629	$6585	$1042
Month 24	1000	425	575	$0	$1885	$6443	$996
Month 25	1000	425	575	$0	$1134	$6301	$951
Month 26	1000	425	575	$0	$375	$6157	$905
Month 27	1000	425	575	$0	$0	$5622	$858
Month 28	1000	230	770	$0	$0	$4705	$812
Month 29	1000	230	770	$0	$0	$3783	$765
Month 30	1000	230	770	$0	$0	$2855	$718
Month 31	1000	230	770	$0	$0	$1921	$671
Month 32	1000	230	770	$0	$0	$983	$624
Month 33	1000	230	770	$0	$0	$38	$577
Month 34	1000	230	770	$0	$0	$0	$0

Note: This is a simplified example and does not account for reduced minimum payments as debts are paid down.

Keep in mind that this can be a much tougher approach when compared to the snowball method, especially if your highest interest debt is associated with your highest balances. There won't be any quick wins using this method. In the example above, it would take 18 months to pay off the first debt – that's a long time before you see any solid results.

Debt Consolidation

When you decide you're ready to start paying back all your debts, you may feel overwhelmed having so many bills to pay at once. Maybe you're feeling confused and mixed up over all the different credit card statements. One way to avoid this issue is to consolidate (combine) that debt into one monthly payment. You can do this by transferring the balances of your different credit cards to a single credit card that has a 0% or very low introductory interest rate.

These low interest rates usually apply for a limited period of time, so it only makes sense if you can pay off your outstanding debt within the timeframe of that introductory rate. You also need to ensure that you carefully read the fine print, so you are aware of any fees associated with the balance transfer. Review everything to make sure the cost of the transfer makes sense.

There are also various organizations that offer debt consolidation services for a small monthly fee. They will call your creditors to negotiate lower interest rates for you and create a payoff timeline for you to follow. If you want to save yourself the monthly fee, call your creditors and negotiate your interest rates yourself. Otherwise, I would suggest you stick to the original plan of paying off each credit card one by one, using one of the methods outlined above.

Calling your creditors to negotiate lower interest rates and creating a payoff plan for yourself might be hard, but being debt free is worth it. Not only will you have more money available to you each month, but you will finally be free of the looming problem.

Tips to Pay Down Debt Fast

For the biggest impact, when it comes to making progress with paying down your debt, here are some key tips and ideas:

- **Develop the right money mindset.** When tackling your debt, having a positive mindset is super-important. It's like giving yourself a pep talk and believing that you've got what it takes to crush that debt. It might take some time, so being mentally prepared is key. Tell yourself things like "I've got this," "Being debt-free is awesome," and "Peace out, debt!" on an ongoing basis. But remember, it's not just about saying these things; you must really believe in them too.
- **Pay more than the minimum.** As I've already mentioned, paying more than the minimum will save you money on monthly interest payments and accelerate how quickly you become debt free. So make it a goal of yours to pay as much as you can each month toward your credit card debt. You'll speed up your repayment and reduce the amount of overall interest you pay to your creditors. It might mean a tighter budget over the short term, but once your debt is gone, you can then reassign that money to your other goals.

- **Use nonretirement or nonemergency savings.** Do you have cash that's sitting in a savings account earning little or no interest? Well, you might want to consider using those funds to pay down your credit card debt.

  All it takes is stepping back and looking at your overall financial picture. If you find that the interest you are paying on your credit cards far exceeds the interest rates you're earning on your savings account, it makes mathematical sense to pay down your debt.

  Once your debt is paid off, you can put the money you would have otherwise been using for credit card payments back toward your savings to build it up again.

  Just remember, always keep your retirement and emergency savings intact. The last thing you want is to have to go back into debt if something unexpected comes up.

- **Consolidate your debt into lower-interest rate payments.** As I mentioned earlier, a good idea might be to consolidate your debt into one monthly payment by transferring the balances from your current credit cards to a new single credit card that has a 0% or very low introductory interest rate.

  For some people, having a single consolidated payment helps them better manage their debt payoff. A lower interest rate will reduce the amount of total interest you pay to your creditors. However, debt consolidation only makes sense if you can pay off your debt within the time frame of the low introductory rate – you don't want to get stuck with all your debt on a high-interest card! You also want to make sure you read the fine print very carefully so you understand the fees and terms associated with transferring your balance, and that it makes financial sense when you crunch the numbers.

- **Sell stuff you no longer use.** A quick way to make some extra cash is by getting rid of electronics, clothing, shoes, and accessories you've never worn or no longer use. You can sell your items online on sites like eBay, Poshmark, or at a local consignment store. Be sure to price your items competitively and review the feedback from potential buyers very carefully before you sell. Once you get that cash, you can apply it directly to your debt.

- **Ask for a raise.** If you've been at your job for a while and think you are due for raise, it's worth having the conversation with your boss to ask for one. Once that raise comes through, you'll want to funnel it directly toward your debt payoff.

- **Start a side hustle.** Do you have a particular skill set that people compliment you on all the time? Or do you have a strong interest in a particular thing? Then maybe it's time you start charging for those skills to earn some extra income. Baking, crafting, graphic design, freelance work – whatever it is, earn some money with your talents and apply it to your debt.

- **Get a part-time job/work overtime.** If running your own side hustle is not your cup of tea, you can consider getting a temporary part-time job or ask for overtime hours if you have that option until your debts are paid off. Be sure to remind yourself why you are working the extra hours – to get rid of your debt. This is only temporary and will totally be worth it in the long run!

- **Cut cable.** Cutting cable can save you a lot of money each month. If you are not an avid sports fan, you might not even miss it at all! Consider switching to an online streaming service like Netflix or Hulu to save some extra cash until your debts are paid off. There's a ton of great content available through streaming services, so pick one or two that you know you'll watch the most. Remember, your goal is to save money, so avoid subscribing to too many services so you don't end up with a big monthly bill!

- **Lower your cell phone plan.** Cell phone plans can get really expensive, especially when it comes to data. Call your service provider to see if there are any specials or offers they can give you for being a loyal customer. Or consider downgrading your plan to one that costs less or switching to another provider altogether if they offer a cheaper plan. We know you need a phone, so don't cancel it entirely, but you can opt for a minimal plan to save some extra cash that will go toward your debt.

- **Take lunch to work every day.** Eating out every day adds up: the average lunch at a restaurant costs between $10 and $15! Instead, plan your lunches for the week based on what you purchase at the grocery store and what you have at home. Take in leftovers from dinner the night before, or specially prepared meals. Either way, you'll save a ton of money by bringing your own food. Pinterest is a great place to get meal planning ideas if you need help coming up with meal options.

- **Skip the movies and nights out for a while.** Movies and nights out also add up. Rather than spending those nights out, try having a special evening in. Make a special meal with your family, your partner, or your friends instead of eating out. Turn on Netflix and pick something exciting instead of popping by the theater.

  Don't want to give up going out? Skip the ridiculously priced popcorn and beverages at the movies and the alcohol on nights out. These items are heavily marked up, and you can put that money toward your debt instead.

- **Carpool.** If you have coworkers who live nearby, see if you can set up a carpool schedule to save money on gas each week – put those savings toward your debt.
- **Cut down on your grocery spending.** Save a few dollars off your grocery bill that can go toward your debt repayment. The easiest way to save money at the grocery store is by making sure you have a list before you go, and a full stomach! This way you don't get sidetracked by what you don't need or whatever food cravings pop up while you're there. Also, look up to see what coupons and sales your store has before you go, and see if you can find manufacturer coupons as well.
- **Cancel unused memberships and subscriptions.** Take a look at your finances and see if you're paying monthly fees for things you don't use. If you barely go to the gym or aren't using a particular subscription, cancel it and put those funds toward your debt. If you're worried that getting rid of your gym membership will mean you won't work out, you can always try working out outdoors or with videos on YouTube.
- **Use tax refunds and bonuses to pay off your debt.** Every year, it's almost inevitable that you'll get some form of extra cash. Whether that's a gift card, a tax rebate, your entire tax return, or a bonus at work, use that extra cash to pay down your debt. Those refunds and bonuses can make a huge impact toward accelerating your debt payoff. I know many people use their tax returns and bonuses to treat themselves – and that can be very tempting – but think of how much happier you'll be with no debt.
- **Automate your payments.** Set up automatic transfers for the amount you've budgeted toward paying off your debt. For example, if you can afford an extra $200 per month, set up a $200 automatic payment to speed up reducing your balance. Automating payments helps avoid late fees and keeps you focused on becoming debt-free!
- **Get an accountability buddy.** Having a like-minded accountability partner is also helpful. They'll support you, keep you motivated, and help you stay on track with your debt payoff and savings goals.

Tackling Your Student Loans

As you start working on your plan to pay off your debt, here are some key tips to keep in mind specifically for your student loans:

- **Be aware of all your student loans and the terms and conditions associated with them.** A lot of young college students sign paperwork they don't quite understand or even remember. In fact, a lot of people don't even know how much they owe and to whom they owe it. If you're in that category, don't worry. Your student loans are recorded on your credit report. If you need the details of your loans, order a free copy of your report today (you can get one at http://annualcreditreport.com) and make sure you know what you owe and to whom.

Once you're aware of all these details, you can create a proper plan around your debt and significantly improve your chances of repayment. Plus, you won't have to deal with surprise debt and interest you didn't realize you owed.

In the process of figuring out the details of your debt, get a copy of your promissory note. Review it to ensure you are aware of the information it contains about the terms and conditions of your loan, including:

- The interest rates on your loans and types of loans you have (Are the interest rates fixed or variable?)
- The interest accrual period
- The details of any in-school, deferment, forbearance, repayment, and postgraduate grace periods
- Your student loan capitalization date (unpaid interest added to your principal balance before your first payment is due)
- Any loan fees, late charges, and collection fees
- How payments on your student loan account will be applied (i.e. how much goes to your principal and how much goes to interest)
- **Factor your student loan payments into your budget and pay more than the minimum.** In addition to paying off your credit card or high-interest debt, your student loans should be on your priority list. The one good thing about student loan debt (if you can call it a good thing) is that interest rates are typically lower than most other types of debt.

  You'll want to make sure your weekly or monthly budget includes your minimum student loan payments plus any extra you can afford to add on each month. Having these loans built into your budget will help you determine if you have any spare money in your budget to apply toward knocking down your principal amounts.
- **Prioritize your student loan payments.** Depending on the interest rates and the terms surrounding your student loans, you can create a priority list to determine which of your loans you'll focus on paying off first. You might choose to focus on paying off the ones with the highest interest rate first or the ones with the highest balance first, or perhaps the ones with the least flexible loan terms. Look back to the snowball and avalanche methods of debt repayment for this part.

Federal student loans usually have lower interest rates than private loans, so you should try to tackle your private loans first if you have both types.

- **Make sure all your additional payments are being applied to your loan principal.** If you are making more than the minimum payments on your student loans (go you!), make sure your additional payments are being applied to your principal and not to the interest. Otherwise, you'll never see your balances go down. Many creditors will apply your payments to interest by default, so double check with them.

   Be sure to review your statements, log in to your accounts, and, if necessary, call your creditors to ensure your additional payments are going toward your principal.

- **Don't skip your student loan payments.** Skipping loan payments just adds to the time it will take to repay and the interest you will have to pay. A lot of times when you graduate, you have a postgraduation grace period, which will allow you to skip payments for a certain amount of time, theoretically while you find a job. However, if you don't have to defer your payments, don't do it. Start making payments as early as you can.

- **Look into student loan forgiveness programs and employee benefit programs.** If you are still in school or you've gone back for grad school, don't wait until you graduate before you start strategizing your student loan payoff. One smart approach is to research student loan forgiveness programs that you may be eligible for and ensure that you thoroughly understand their requirements.

   The Federal Student Aid website (https://studentaid.ed.gov/sa) provides information on federal forgiveness programs available for federal student loans. That would be a good place to start. Keep in mind, however, that the federal government is not the only one in the student loan forgiveness business. Make sure to research loan forgiveness programs at the state and local level as well.

   When it comes to employee benefits, some employers offer student loan repayment benefits as a perk. Be sure to inquire about this and take full advantage if your employer can make this available to you.

- **Don't stop saving for your future self.** Once you have a plan in place for your student loans, don't stop saving for your future self. Pay yourself first, even if it means contributing just a small percentage of your income to your retirement savings while you focus on tackling your debt. Also, if your employer offers a match on your retirement contributions, take it. It's essentially free money and an immediate 100% return on your contributions.

Explore Scholarships

If you're still in school, are planning to pursue an additional degree or certification, or plan to pay for a child's college education, it's worth exploring scholarship options because a wide variety exist. Here are some places to start:

- The financial aid section on the websites of the colleges and universities you are interested in applying to or already attend
- Websites like bigfuture.collegeboard.org/scholarship-search, Appily.com, Fastweb.com, and Scholarships.com
- Inquiring about scholarship options from your employers
- Professional associations and organizations related to your career path that provide scholarships to specific fields or industries
- The Federal Student Aid (FAFSA) portal from the U.S. Department of Education for federal scholarships and grants (studentaid.gov/understand-aid/types/scholarships)
- Your state government education agency for scholarships specific to your state (www2.ed.gov/about/contacts/state)

Checklist: Stay on Top of Your Student Loans

☐	Have your student loan account numbers, initial amount borrowed, interest rates, and lender information documented and easily accessible.
☐	Get a copy of your loan amortization schedule and payment information.
☐	Pull your loan history and check your credit report to confirm what loans are listed.
☐	Review and understand: • How your payments will be allocated toward fees, interest, and principal • Your lender's customer service standards and procedures on delinquency, defaults, and deferments • Your lender's options for deferment • Your lender's policies and procedures on refinancing and consolidating your loans
☐	Create a debt prioritization and payment plan including your student loans.

☐	Set up online payments for your loans to easily track and manage your loans.
☐	Review every statement you receive and pay close attention to the details around your principal balance and unpaid interest balance.
☐	Look into any forgiveness programs and employee benefit programs that you may be eligible for.
☐	If you're still in school, are planning to pursue an additional degree or certification, or plan to pay for a child's college education, explore scholarship options.

Now it's time to lay out your debt priority and repayment plan.

Selected debt payoff method:_____

Debt Prioritization Worksheet

	Debt name/ Creditor	Current balance	Interest rate (%)	Minimum monthly payment	Extra monthly payment	Months to payoff
1						
2						
3						
4						
5						
6						
7						
8						
9						
10						
11						
12						
13						

	Debt name/ Creditor	Current balance	Interest rate (%)	Minimum monthly payment	Extra monthly payment	Months to payoff
14						
15						
16						
17						
18						
19						
20						

Note: To download printable pdf and Excel versions of the debt prioritization worksheet, visit http://clevergirlfinance.com/my-wealth-plan.

You can also **download the Clever Girl Finance Debt Reduction Calculator** at http://clevergirlfinance.com/my-wealth-plan. It will help you lay out your debt payoff plan based on the debt payoff method you choose to use.

CHAPTER 13

Your Credit

When was the last time you checked your credit? Is everything on your credit report documented accurately? Are all your bills being paid on time? Are you aware of any delinquencies? You should be able to answer all of these questions about your credit at any point in time. This way, you know your status before you apply for loans. That said, let's first break things down:

Your credit score or creditworthiness is used to determine your eligibility for pay-to-use services like a cell phone contract or your apartment rental and is used to determine your interest rate and credit limits on your credit cards and loans. Some employers may also use your credit report as a determining factor when considering you for a job.

Your credit history is a record of how well you've paid your bills in the past and is used to determine your credit score. Financial institutions like banks and loan brokers report the amounts of money you owe, your track record for making payments, and any delinquencies on your accounts. Then various credit agencies use this information to determine your creditworthiness – or how risky it is to loan you money.

A credit report, on the other hand, is documentation of your credit history over time. This is basically a record of everything in your credit history.

In the United States, there are three major credit bureaus: Equifax, Transunion, and Experian. Their main job is to collect your credit information from various sources, aggregate them into a report, assign you a credit score, and make this information available to your potential lenders.

Knowing your credit score and what's in your credit history will also help you identify credit fraud or identity theft and resolve it if it happens to you – this is very important to catch early. Leaving issues like this over a long term will ruin your credit and can be a royal pain to fix.

Remember, you should use credit wisely and to your advantage, like for a home loan, getting a cell phone, renting an apartment, or acquiring business financing. These are all uses that will (most likely) benefit you now or in the future. Avoid racking up credit card debt, which, over the long term, costs too much and benefits you very little.

When it comes to your credit, the key to maintaining a great credit score is never to miss your bill payments. Avoid paying late or paying less than the minimum required. For credit cards, plan to pay your balance in full each month.

If you're intentional and objective about the way you use credit, you'll be sure to maintain a great credit score. This gives you a great advantage when it comes time to negotiate interest rates on all kinds of credit, including your credit cards and your mortgage. Keeping on top of your credit report and consistently checking to ensure the information is accurate will help you mitigate problems with identity theft or credit fraud. Now that you're clear on the basics, let's get into the details of credit scores.

Checking Your Credit Report

A lot of people are not aware of this, but in the United States, you are entitled to a free credit report from each of the three credit bureaus (Experian, Equifax, and Transunion) once every year. You can order these free reports online at http://annualcreditreport.com.

Improving Your Credit Score

According to http://myfico.com, a "good" credit score is between 670 and 739, while a credit score between 740 and 799 is considered "very good."[1]

This means that you'll more than likely be approved for a loan at the best possible interest rate. So, ideally, your goal should be to get as close to these ranges as possible. In addition to qualifying for better interest rates, improving your credit score makes you more attractive to lenders, landlords, and even some employers.

In order to improve your credit score, you need to make sure you know what is currently on your credit report, pay all your bills and loans on time, and reduce your overall debt-to-credit ratio by paying down debt.

---

[1] https://www.myfico.com/credit-education/credit-scores

Regardless of your credit card limits, you want to keep your credit card balances to the minimum and pay them off in full each month.

Rebuilding or Maintaining Your Credit

Again, according to http://myfico.com, a score of 580 or lower is considered "poor credit," while a score between 580 and 669 is considered "fair."[2] If your credit score falls anywhere in this area and you need to secure some sort of financing in the near future (i.e. for a house or a car), you should be concerned about improving your credit score.

As I've mentioned, having good credit means you can get the best available interest rates when it comes to credit and financing. It also lets landlords and employers know how you handle bill payments and therefore demonstrates how responsible you are with money. Clearly, having good credit is important, so let's look at a few ways you can work to improve your rating:

- **Get a copy of your current credit report from all three credit bureaus.** First things first, you want to know where you currently stand with your credit. You need to understand what has been reported about you, how much you owe, your different account types, and any late payments or delinquencies that have been recorded. Once you understand what has been reported, you can dispute any inconsistencies and have those issues removed from your record.
- **Pay your bills on time; catch up on your payments.** Paying your bills on time proves your creditworthiness to lenders and has a huge impact on your credit score. If you are behind on any payments, you need to get caught up as soon as you can. Call your creditors, create payment plans, and set up new payment dates.

  Set reminders for yourself for all your bills to make sure you don't forget to make any payments in the future.
- **Pay down your debt.** Your overall debt load, as well as your percentage of credit utilization, affects your credit score. Let's say you have a credit card with a limit of $1000 and you owe $950 on it; your utilization is 95%. This high utilization can count against you because creditors use it as a gauge to see how likely you are to pay back what you owe.

  A high utilization makes you less attractive to a creditor, so reducing your debt load can increase your score immensely. Keep in mind that the goal of paying down your debt shouldn't just be for

---

[2] https://www.myfico.com/credit-education/credit-scores

a good credit rating. By paying down debt, you save yourself tons of money in interest payments that you can then put toward long-term savings and investing.

- **Avoid too many new credit applications over a short period of time.** Applying to and opening too many new lines of credit over a short period of time can have a negative impact on your credit. When you apply for new credit, lenders will typically run a hard inquiry on your credit report, which can lower your score slightly for a short period of time.

  Additionally, multiple credit applications in a short timeframe might make lenders think you have money troubles and raise concerns about your ability to pay back the debt. So space out your credit applications (it's a good idea to wait six months between applications), and only apply for new lines of credit when you really need to. This will show lenders you are responsible with credit.

- **Don't close your old credit card accounts.** Your credit card accounts make up a vital part of your credit report, specifically your credit history. If you have accounts that show you've been paying your bills on time consistently, keep them as part of your credit history.

  If they are accounts you have paid off, keep them open and make the occasional small purchase on them and then pay it off in full each month. If they are accounts you are actively paying off, over time those on-time payments will positively impact your overall credit score and reduce your credit utilization. If you do decide to close your account for a specific reason, be sure to pay down any other credit card balances you have first to avoid an increase in your overall credit utilization rate. This is because once you close a credit card account, it reduces your overall available credit across all your lines of credit, which in turn can impact your debt-to-credit ratio.

- **Be smart about your finances.** Pay off and avoid debt, build an emergency fund, save for retirement, check your credit frequently – these are all things you should be doing over the long term. Establishing good financial habits ensures you avoid scenarios that will impact your credit.

  When you take care of your finances, your credit score should improve. As you automate your bill payments and include them in your budget, you ensure all your accounts are up to date. As you pay down your debt, your credit utilization decreases. These two factors, along with the positive credit history you'll be building, will ensure your credit score continues to increase, leaving you with much better opportunities for accessing credit in the future.

While maintaining a good credit score is important, you'll want to pay extra attention to this if you intend to buy a house or apply for a business loan in the near future.

To make sure you are on top of your credit, here is a checklist of a few things you can do:

Staying on Top of Your Credit Checklist

☐	Pull your credit reports and review them in detail. You can get a free copy of your report from all three credit bureaus at http://annualcreditreport.com.
☐	Put monitoring on your credit so you are aware of any changes that occur, including any fraudulent activity or attempts. Note that your credit score may vary from one app to another depending on the scoring methodology they use.
☐	Dispute errors on your credit report in writing. Review your credit reports from all three credit bureaus in detail to check for errors. If you find an error, be sure to contact the bureau immediately and also dispute it in writing.
☐	Address outstanding debt or debt in collections. This means contacting your creditors and coming to a payment agreement so you can start resolving the debt ASAP. Also ask if negative remarks can be removed once you pay off your debt. Depending on the creditor, sometimes they will do it.

CHAPTER **14**

Protecting Yourself (Insurance)

Although most people don't like thinking about it, bad things can and do happen in life. Your basement could flood, or you could become ill. What about a car accident or, God forbid, a death in your family? They aren't pleasant to think about, but the truth is that you need to ensure you protect yourself against these possibilities.

Having the right insurance can potentially save you a ton of money in the event of an emergency or unplanned life occurrence. It means you can protect yourself without having to impact your financial plans or offset your goal timelines. On the flipside, not having adequate insurance can derail your financial goals, and you don't want that!

Although insurance can often feel like an unnecessary cost – especially if you've never had to use it – you'll find that over the course of your life, you'll be thankful, at least once, that you had it. But what's challenging about insurance is knowing exactly what you need and what will be covered. In this section, I'll outline several types of insurance you should consider getting. You can then use the worksheet at the end of this section to determine any insurance gaps you need to fill.

Health Insurance

In the United States, the cost of healthcare is high, so having health insurance is necessary. Seeing a doctor can run you anywhere from

$100 to $300 out of pocket for an initial consultation – or more if you need a procedure done or require serious medical attention.

According to the Peterson-KFF Health System Tracker (healthsystemtracker.org), depending on where you are located and at the time of this writing, the costs associated with pregnancy, childbirth, and postpartum care average $4768 for a regular delivery to upwards of $26,280 or more for a C-section before any insurance coverage. With insurance coverage, the average out-of-pocket expense for a regular delivery is $2655 and for a C-section it's $3214.[1] Having health insurance allows you to get the right care when you need it and reduce the financial burden of having to pay completely out of pocket because instead you'll only have to pay a co-pay.

Many employers offer health insurance plans to employees. If this is available to you, look into it and take advantage if it makes financial sense. If nothing is offered where you work, there are plenty of private plans that offer great coverage. The federal government website (https://finder .healthcare.gov/) can help you find private healthcare options for various budgets and needs.

Auto Insurance

First of all, not having auto insurance in the United States is illegal and punishable by law. If you own a car, you must have auto insurance. However, you can get coverage above and beyond the legal minimums if you want extra coverage. Not only does auto insurance cover the cost of repairs incurred from a car accident after you meet the deductible requirements, but it also covers hospital bills you or the other driver might incur, rental cars if yours will be out of commission, and protection against legal action.

If you currently pay for the legal minimum in auto insurance, look into additional coverage. You might find the benefits offered are advantageous to your particular situation.

Renter's Insurance

If you are renting your home, you are not responsible for the actual building or major repairs. However, you may want to consider getting

---

[1]https://www.healthsystemtracker.org/brief/health-costs-associated-with-pregnancy-childbirth-and-postpartum-care/

renter's insurance to cover the valuables you keep at home in the event that they ever get damaged by flooding, fire, or another disaster – or in the event that your home is broken into. This type of insurance would cover electronics and other valuables and is very affordable.

Homeowner's Insurance

If you own a home, insurance is essential. Imagine if you had to rebuild your house or replace everything you have in your home out of pocket. That could be financially devastating! Plus, if you've financed your home with a mortgage, insurance on your home was likely required in order to close. This type of insurance protects your home against damages to the house itself and to possessions within the home in the case of a theft or damage from a natural disaster. If you live in an area prone to flooding or tornados, you can add on specific natural disaster insurance to your insurance coverage to further protect your home.

Insuring Your Home-Based Business or Home Office

If you have a home-based business or a home office and you already have homeowner's insurance, be sure that your policy covers your business and all the equipment in your home office. You can also get independent business or office insurance that will provide you with coverage as well. This way, in the event of damage or a burglary, your business is still protected.

Protecting Your Home Against Burglary

No one ever wants it to happen to them, but burglaries and break-ins do occur. In fact, in the United States there are about 1.7 million of them every year. Clearly, it's a good idea to protect your home from these situations. Consider getting an alarm system installed (you may qualify for discounts on your insurance policy if you have one), make sure there is good lighting at your entryway, and install strong locks or deadbolts on your doors.

In addition, be sure to check all your windows frequently to make sure they are locked when you are not home or you are sleeping. Also consider buying a safe to store things like important documents and jewelry in your home – bonus points if it's fireproof and waterproof!

Life Insurance

Although it's not necessary for everyone, life insurance is something to consider if you have dependents. For example, if your income is essential to your family's welfare, or if you have children or other major financial commitments, you will benefit from having life insurance. The main purpose of life insurance is to provide a lump-sum payment to your dependents in the event of your death. Life insurance is often thought to be quite complicated because of the different types you can buy and the varying amounts of coverage. In reality, what you need might be quite simple.

- **Term life insurance:** You pay an annual premium according to the amount of coverage you want. In the event of your death, your beneficiaries are paid a lump sum. Usually, you'd take your annual income and multiply it by the number of years you want your family to be covered.
- **Cash value insurance (e.g. universal or whole life):** This is a combination of your standard life insurance and some sort of cash value feature. With this type of insurance, the longer you pay, the more money your beneficiaries receive. You can also leverage your built-up cash value. While this type of life insurance sounds attractive, it is also more expensive, so you'll want to keep that in mind.

Regardless of what type of life insurance you choose, you want to make sure you fully understand what is associated with each, how much coverage the premium provides, and if there are any conditions or requirements that must be met before you can benefit.

Long-Term Disability Insurance

This insurance covers you by replacing your income in the event that you are unable to work due to a permanent or temporary disability. Whether or not you have dependents, if you have monthly living expenses, then you definitely want to look into getting disability insurance.

If you determine this is right for you, look into the requirements for approval, which disabilities are covered, and how much you will benefit for the premium you pay. Not all insurance is equal.

Personal Article Insurance

Got an expensive engagement ring or wedding ring set? A one-of-a-kind watch? A laptop you take with you everywhere? If you have any

personal items that are of value that you often have with you outside of your home, consider insuring them through a personal articles
policy. This type of insurance covers theft, damage, and loss of expensive items.

Pet Insurance

If you're a pet person, pet insurance can be beneficial. Medical care for
your pets can be incredibly expensive if they are injured or diagnosed
with an illness. Because they are a part of your family, you'll want to
be sure you can give them the best care possible. Keep in mind that as
your pet gets older, the more medical attention they might need. Having this type of insurance will save you from going broke to take care
of your family pet.

With all of that said, remember that not all insurance is necessary.
It can sound really nice to have coverage for any and all possibilities,
but the reality is that insurance can turn out to be pretty pricey. You'll
want to make sure that whatever additional insurance coverage you
get fits into your budget and makes sense for your life situation. You
also want to be sure that the potential payout from an insurance policy
far outweighs the cost you'll be paying to have the coverage over time.

**Use the following worksheet to assess the insurance you
currently have and still need.**

Insurance type	Insurance provider	Contact info (website, phone, or email)	Premium amount (per month or per year)	Renewal date	Current (Yes or No)
Health					
Auto					
Renters					

Insurance type	Insurance provider	Contact info (website, phone, or email)	Premium amount (per month or per year)	Renewal date	Current (Yes or No)
Homeowners					
Life					
Disability					
Personal article					
Home warranty					
_____					
_____					
_____					
_____					

Based on the worksheet you just completed:

1. Review your various insurance policies to determine what's covered and if there are any gaps you want to fill.
2. Make some time to inquire about extra coverage, new policies, and even new providers.
3. Make note of future insurance needs you might have based on upcoming life changes.

CHAPTER **15**

Asking for More Money

When I graduated from college and got my first job, my starting salary was $54,000. I was ecstatic. It was more money than I'd ever earned in my life, and as far I was concerned, I was balling. It didn't once cross my mind to ask for more money or even a signing bonus. I was just happy I got a job.

Well, as time went by and I got to know my coworkers, I realized that I was the lowest earner in the entire group, despite all being hired for the same position – and despite the fact that we all had similar educational backgrounds.

Some of them made thousands of dollars more than I did, while others had gotten signing bonuses. Why? Because unlike me, they didn't accept the first offer they received. Instead, they asked for more. Not only did asking for more get them more money, but it also positioned them to earn more when it came time for raises and bonuses, since those are given as a percentage of the base salary. Over the course of their careers, that's likely hundreds of thousands of dollars more than I'd make.

That experience lit a fire in me to step out of my comfort zone and get what I knew I was worth going forward. And so, knowing what I know now, being older and wiser, I have four quick tips to help you become a better negotiator and get what you are truly worth:

- **Don't be afraid to ask.** Fear is the number-one reason we don't ask for more money – but what are we really afraid of? The worst thing that could possibly happen is that the request is rejected, and that's it. So instead of being afraid or intimidated, come up with a plan on how to make your request.

Practice your spiel in front of the mirror, type it up and read it out loud, and then ask yourself, "What's the worst thing that could possibly happen?" Understanding that your request for a raise is not a life-or-death matter will help you put things in perspective and put your fear back in its place.

With each new job I got, not only did I negotiate my base salary, I also negotiated other benefits as well, including more vacation days, the option to work from home, a better work computer, and even a better ergonomic office chair! The worst response I got was "no" and so I would simply shelve my request and revisit it a few months later after I had accomplished something big at work.

- **Treat your request like a business transaction.** As women, we tend to tie our emotions to the things that go on in our lives, including our careers and asking for raises. When our emotions are involved, we sometimes tend to show vulnerability or look like we are complaining because we've associated our feelings with the situation. Keep in mind that a request for a raise might not come across the way you want it to.

  To get around this, know that it's all about your delivery. When you make your request, don't make any excuses or complaints. Instead, think of it as a business transaction – present your case and why you deserve a raise, talk about your accomplishments, and keep it strictly business. Try as much as you can to keep your emotions and complaints to a minimum.

  For me, it helped to schedule a formal meeting with my boss to have these kinds of conversations. Beforehand, I would outline my talking points so I could go into the meeting prepared to have a focused discussion.

- **Leverage what makes you unique and valuable.** Know your professional worth and capitalize on it! When you make your request, talk about the value you've brought to the company. Remind your boss what you've accomplished, created, or improved and the success that your work has driven. When you present your case this way, they'll be hard-pressed to turn you down.

  So start keeping a list of all your accomplishments and successes at work, no matter how small. This way when it comes round to speaking with your boss or completing a self-assessment, you have this list of all the great work you've done as a reference.

- **Do your research.** When asking for a raise, it's important to be realistic. Do your research and understand what the industry averages are for your role and location. Don't expect to be given anything if you don't know what you're worth. But also, be sure you're not asking for a salary fit for a major city if you're in a small town.

  With each new job I got, I also made sure to ask what it would take for me to qualify for the next highest possible raise and the highest possible bonus when the time for raises and bonuses came around, so I knew what to focus on and where to improve.

Prepare for your next salary negotiation conversation with the following checklist:

Salary Negotiation Prep Checklist

Do research to determine competitive salary rates in your city and industry:	
☐	Use sites like Glassdoor, LinkedIn, and PayScale.
☐	Reach out to people you know in similar industries for insights.
☐	If this data is available, look up your target company's financial health and salary trends.
☐	Determine the minimum acceptable salary you would be happy with.
☐	Determine your ideal salary range.
☐	Compare these numbers (minimum acceptable salary versus ideal salary) with industry standards and your research findings.
Other negotiable areas:	
☐	Paid time off (PTO)
☐	Health insurance
☐	Retirement plans
☐	Remote work options
☐	Flexible hours
☐	Professional development: training programs, educational reimbursement, etc.

Create a negotiation strategy to justify your salary request:
☐	List your relevant skills, experience, and accomplishments.
☐	Highlight specific examples where you've added value to previous employers.
☐	Explain what makes you uniquely qualified for this role.
☐	Have a strategy for counteroffers or compromise.
Lay out your plan B:
☐	Have a strategy for counteroffers or compromise.
☐	Plan how you will continue the job search or negotiate with other potential employers if you chose to walk away.

CHAPTER **16**

Your Self-Care

Your self-care and your finances are interconnected in so many ways. For instance, by maintaining good physical and mental health through things like exercising regularly, eating a balanced diet, and good stress management, you can minimize the need for medical interventions, and in turn minimize or avoid expensive healthcare costs.

Practicing self-care also means that you are setting boundaries because you are specifically allocating time for rest and relaxation. This can prevent burnout and improve your overall well-being, which can be extremely helpful for focusing on your goals and making sound decisions – including your money goals and financial decisions.

And did you know that practicing self-care can help you avoid impulse spending? That's right! Self-care doesn't mean spending a ton of money on products and fads. In fact, it can help you save. By doing things that make you happy and relaxed, you're less likely to be driven by stress to blow cash on random stuff you never planned to purchase in the first place. It's like your emotions are in check, so your wallet stays in line too.

Plus, being top of your self-care game – taking breaks, getting enough sleep, and not letting stress run your life – can boost your productivity and performance at work or in your business, which can lead to higher income and, when managed correctly, an increased sense of financial stability.

Now that you know the importance of self-care and how it ties into your personal finances, here are some simple practices I do that you can start implementing as well.

Do a Digital Detox

Give your eyes and mind a break from screens. Schedule regular digital detox sessions so you can reduce your screen time and reconnect with the real world around you. Your brain will thank you for the breather. One way I do this easily is by sometimes leaving my phone at home when I'm going out for a few hours.

Practice Mindfulness

Take a few minutes each day to pause and just be in the moment. Whether it's enjoying your morning coffee, sitting outside on a warm day, or writing in a journal, these little pauses can reset your mind and ease stress.

Get Moving

Find something active that brings you joy. Whether it's dancing in your living room, hiking, or doing yoga, keeping your body active is a win-win for your mood and your health. I try to work out at home three to four times a week and I alternate between strength and cardio. I've found so many great workout channels on YouTube; one of my favorite channels is "Grow with Jo."

Eat Well

Eat meals that keep you full for longer, drink lots of water, and give yourself permission to have that occasional treat you love without feeling guilty. I'm not big on diets or food trends; instead I focus on moderation. I also carry a reusable water bottle with me almost everywhere I go so I'm constantly reminded to drink more water!

Stay Connected

Spending quality time with your friends or family can be a great mood booster. Whether it's a coffee date with a friend or a cozy movie night in with loved ones, these moments are great to keep your spirit up. Sometimes this can be hard to do, especially if you have a busy or hectic life, so I have a monthly calendar reminder on my phone to reach out to a friend I haven't see in a while to schedule a meetup.

Schedule Dedicated "Me Time"

Set aside dedicated time each week for activities that you enjoy and that recharge your batteries. It could be reading a book, taking a long bath, or simply lounging without any distractions. My dedicated me time happens on Fridays. My kids are usually in school, I don't schedule any meetings, and I get to spend time doing simple things that make me happy, like getting a pedicure, taking a long walk, or spending a couple of hours at the bookstore.

Get Enough Sleep

Set a bedtime and stick to it. You can even establish your own bedtime routine. I love to wind down with a warm shower, some skin care, and listening to or reading a good book. It's like a signal to my body that once this happens, bedtime is soon.

Seek Support or Guidance if You Need To

If you're feeling overwhelmed or need extra support, there's absolutely no shame in reaching out to a trusted friend or a professional. Sometimes, just being able to share what's weighing you down with someone you trust can help you feel so much better. Therapy can also be a game-changer in helping you navigate life's ups and downs with grace and resilience. Many workplace insurance policies cover therapy, so it's worth exploring.

Don't Forget Gratitude

Gratitude isn't just about how it makes us feel; it also can also attract positive opportunities and relationships. How, you ask? Well, by practicing gratitude, you are more likely to approach challenges and setbacks with a positive attitude and come up with creative solutions. Gratitude also helps you create a mindset that can recognize opportunities when they come your way, as opposed to dismissing them because you are focused on what you don't have. People also love to be around those who radiate positive energy, and that's exactly what being grateful does for you.

So reminding ourselves to be grateful daily is like unlocking a secret power that brings a ton of positivity to everything we do. I keep a daily gratitude journal where I write down one to three things that I'm grateful for each day. This exercise makes me pause and think about all the good I have going on in my life each day, which in turn helps me reframe my thinking. It is especially helpful when I've had a rough day. I highly recommend keeping a gratitude list.

Here are some questions you can ask yourself to create or assess your self-care practices.

Am I:

Y/N

	Getting enough rest?
	Eating well (i.e. balanced meals)?
	Staying active/incorporating movement into my daily routine?
	Prioritizing my mental wellness?
	Making time for the things that bring me joy?
	Giving myself grace and being self-compassionate?
	Setting boundaries in my relationship and with work to protect my peace?
	Saying no to noncritical commitments that overwhelm me?
	Practicing gratitude?
	Do I need to seek support or guidance when dealing with challenging emotions or situations?

What stressors am I currently facing, and how am I currently managing them?

Based on your responses to the previous checklist and question, what specific actions can you take and/or routines can you put in place to take better care of yourself? Set specific timelines to get started.

PART II

Investing

Outside the United States?

If you are outside the United States, be sure to research investments in your country or speak to a licensed financial advisor.

CHAPTER 17

Your Investing Mindset

The way you think about investing makes all the difference in whether or not you'll actually become a successful investor. That's why I believe it's so important first to adjust your mindset around investing, especially if you've had any negative thoughts or feelings toward it in the past. The last thing you want is for your own thoughts to be the roadblock in the way of the success you can achieve.

Some common things many of us tell ourselves about why we can't or shouldn't invest include:

- Investing is too hard. I could never learn how to do it.
- Investing is only for rich people. They have extra money to burn.
- Investing is the same as gambling. I might as well hit the slots in Vegas.
- Investing is scary and I work too hard for my money to take those types of risks.

Do any of the above statements sound familiar? In the past when you've thought about investing, you may have felt anxious, overwhelmed, confused, or stressed out. Well, girlfriend, let's change that.

Here's the truth:

- *Yes*, investing can be hard to do, but it doesn't *have* to be if you have the right plan and strategy in place specific to your unique needs.
- *Yes*, rich people invest their money. For the most part, this is how they've built their wealth. But so can you! With commitment, discipline, and knowledge, you can even join the ranks of the wealthy yourself.

- *Yes*, many consider investing a gamble. And it certainly can be if you don't know what you're doing! But since you're reading this book, you're definitely not about that "gambling away your hard-earned money" life. And yes, you work really hard for your money, spending hours commuting to work, working on tasks and projects, attending meetings, dealing with bosses and colleagues. It makes sense that you'd be apprehensive about investing after all the work you've had to put in to earn it. But in reality, investing is a way to make the most of that money and enable yourself to work less.

Why Investing Matters

When you save your money in a bank account, you'll never be able to earn much more than the amount you save.

But as an investor, you can earn money from:

- **Appreciation:** This is what happens when the invested assets you own increase in value.
- **Interest payments:** This is money you earn from buying investments like bonds, where you lend money to a corporation or to the government and they guarantee interest in return.
- **Dividends:** These are payments that companies issue to their stockholders based on profits earned.

Because there are multiple ways to earn money by investing, there is the opportunity for you to diversify your investments and earnings. As you continue doing this over time, your money earns money, and then *that* money earns money (this is called *compounding*), so we are talking about potential exponential growth here. This can all multiply far beyond what you are able to earn by exchanging your time for money and putting it in a savings account. Not to worry, we'll be getting into more details on how all of this works later.

So why does investing matter?

Investing matters because regardless of how you do it, it's the one way in which you can put your money to work for you so you can increase your income without increasing your workload and build the life you truly desire. If you've ever thought about retiring early into the lap of luxury, traveling the world with loved ones, owning a beautiful home or even multiple homes, having the freedom to work on your passions, being able to be generous with loved ones and charities, or any other dream that money can empower you to achieve, then investing is how you get there. If you're wondering how the truly rich get and stay rich, investing is the answer. That's right – no magic tricks!

Whatever doubts you've had about investing in the past, let them go. You are taking a new path here – one that is going to equip you with everything you need to be a successful investor.

So let's get started with adjusting your investing mindset.

In the first column of the next worksheet, write down every fear or negative thought you have when it comes to investing. It can be based on your past experiences with investing if you've had any, or simply based on what you've heard from others or seen in the media. For example, one could be "I'm worried I'll lose my money in a recession."

In the second column, write down all the things you wish you knew or would like to learn about investing that would help you counter each of the fears you've written down. Using our same example of a recession, the thing to learn could be "How to respond to a recession while investing."

Keep this list handy as you go through this investing section of the workbook. Check off the items you learn as you go along and cross out the fears next to them in the process. The more you know, the more confident you'll be as an investor and the fewer fears you'll have.

Negative thoughts about investing/Investing fears	Counters (What I wish I knew/What I would like to learn about investing)	Progress made? (Yes/No)
		☐
		☐
		☐

Negative thoughts about investing/Investing fears	Counters (What I wish I knew/What I would like to learn about investing)	Progress made? (Yes/No)
		☐
		☐
		☐
		☐
		☐
		☐

CHAPTER **18**

Preparing to Invest

As you start to think about investing now and into the future, it's important to understand the direct impact the economy and stock market have on your investments. The behavior of the economy can affect your portfolio in several ways, including:

- **Through inflation.** Inflation is essentially the increased costs of goods and services and the decline of the purchasing power that money has. For instance, inflation can cause the same exact product (like bread or milk) to cost more today than it did five years ago. High inflation reduces the purchasing power of the dollar, so $50 now will buy you fewer groceries than it used to. Since high inflation can make it expensive to buy goods and services, it discourages consumers from making as many purchases. This causes companies to have lower sales and in turn less revenue, in which case their stock value could fall. On the other hand, low inflation means people have more spending power and companies are doing well with sales and revenue, which in turn causes their stock value to rise. This rise and fall of stocks in relation to inflation directly affects your portfolio because if the value of a stock you own falls, your investment is worth less, and if the value of the stock increases, your investment is worth more in turn.

- **Through changes in interest rates.** Interest rate targets are set by the Federal Reserve. These interest rates help determine what it costs to borrow money from your bank, credit card company, or other type of lender, as well as how much interest you're paid (e.g. in a savings account). Banks and lenders can still set their own specific rates, which is why you will find higher and lower interest rates from different institutions, but usually they will all respond in some way to changes in Federal Reserve targets. Typically, interest rates are raised in strong economies to manage excessiveness and lowered in declining economies to encourage spending.

When interest rates increase or decrease, the value of stock prices can be indirectly affected as well. For example, if interest rates are increased, the interest rate on mortgages for prospective home buyers will be higher. In turn, monthly mortgage payments will also be higher. When people have higher mortgage payments, they also have less discretionary income to spend, which can impact the sales and revenues of businesses that are publicly traded in the stock market. In turn, of course, the value of their stock and your portfolio can decline.

- **During bear markets.** A "bear market" is a term commonly mentioned when the stock market is being discussed. Basically, during bear markets, stock prices are in decline, and this makes investors nervous. (The name literally makes me think of bears hibernating in caves; the economy is just hibernating, too!) A bear market usually goes hand in hand with a flat or declining economy. Often, investors see these declining prices, panic, and sell their stocks, often at a loss, because they're afraid of further declines. Panicking, however, is not a good idea, especially when you have time on your side and can weather the storm. In fact, a bear market could present great opportunities to buy stocks that are undervalued. In other words, it could be described as "the stock market on sale," because when stock prices are lower, you can buy them for cheaper. A bear market is a great time to revisit your financial objectives and make sure they're right for you.

- **During bull markets.** This is another commonly mentioned term. If a bear market is hibernating, a bull market is charging. During bull markets, stock prices rise, investors gain confidence because their investments are making money, and as a result they are motivated to buy, buy, buy. And who doesn't love that?! Bull markets are typically high-growth times.

- **During market bubbles.** In market bubbles, stocks are typically overvalued, and prices of stocks are much higher than they are worth. The bubble eventually bursts, as all bubbles do, and prices fall. Bubbles usually occur with "hot" investments when everyone is rushing to buy and inflating the actual value of the investment. A good example of this was the real estate bubble that burst, causing the 2008 financial crisis and recession due to overvalued real estate, easy access to financing (even when people could not afford it), and a lot of speculative behavior on the part of investors. Investors who buy "hot" investments at the height of a bubble usually lose the most. Unfortunately, the impact of market bubbles in specific industries can trickle into other industries and markets. For instance, the 2008 recession had a global impact. So, when it comes to investing, relying on hot stocks is not the way to go.

In summary, when it comes to the economy's behavior and how it impacts your investments, the goal is to ensure your overall portfolio is well-diversified and you have clear objectives and a simple yet effective long-term strategy to build wealth regardless of bears, bulls, or bubbles.

Compounding

When it comes to investing, compounding helps your investments earn more money as the value of your investment goes up. Compounding can take effect in the following ways:

- **Through interest.** Compounding can amplify any interest earned on your investments based on a rate of return. The rate of return (RoR) is the average profit the investment achieves (or is expected to achieve) over a specified time period and is usually depicted as a percentage. This interest is added to your original investment, which in turn can continue to compound at a larger scale over time.
- **Through dividends.** This is a portion of earnings paid by companies to their shareholders based on stock performance. Your dividends can be reinvested on top of your original investment, which in turn will allow for an increased compounding rate.
- **Through capital gains.** These are any profits you earn when you sell an investment. These earnings can then be used toward another investment to take advantage of the power of compounding.

Let's look at a couple of examples showcasing how compounding works using interest.

Example 1

Let's say you start investing $5000 a year (or $416.67 a month) at the age of 25 with a goal to retire about 40 years later once you turn 65. We'll assume an average return of 6% (average meaning inclusive of the stock market's declines and growth).

After 40 years and with the power of compounding, your investment would be worth **$820,238,42**. If had you just put your
money in a savings account for 40 years at a bank savings interest rate of 0.09%, you'd only have **$203,551,98**. Maybe instead
you decide to save with a high-interest online bank and get 2%
interest; then after 40 years, you'd still only have **$302,012,33**.

The table illustrates what would happen if you kept investing
$5000 a year. The first column is the total amount of your contri-
butions over time, the second column is the amount of interest/
growth alone you'll have earned since beginning to invest, and
the third is the two added together for the total portfolio value you
could have by each age.

Age	Total contributions	Rate of return (6%)	Total
25	$ 5000	$ 300	$ 5300,00
26	$ 10,000	$ 918	$ 10,918,00
27	$ 15,000	$ 1873,08	$ 16,873,08
28	$ 20,000	$ 3185,46	$ 23,185,46
29	$ 25,000	$ 4876,59	$ 29,876,59
30	$ 30,000	$ 6969,19	$ 36,969,19
31	$ 35,000	$ 9487,34	$ 44,487,34
32	$ 40,000	$ 12,456,58	$ 52,456,58
33	$ 45,000	$ 15,903,97	$ 60,903,97
34	$ 50,000	$ 19,858,21	$ 69,858,21
35	$ 55,000	$ 24,349,71	$ 79,349,71
36	$ 60,000	$ 29,410,69	$ 89,410,69
37	$ 65,000	$ 35,075,33	$100,075,33
38	$ 70,000	$ 41,379,85	$ 111,379,85
39	$ 75,000	$ 48,362,64	$123,362,64
40	$ 80,000	$ 56,064,40	$136,064,40
41	$ 85,000	$ 64,528,26	$149,528,26
42	$ 90,000	$ 73,799,96	$163,799,96
43	$ 95,000	$ 83,927,96	$ 178,927,96
44	$100,000	$ 94,963,63	$194,963,63

Age	Total contributions	Rate of return (6%)	Total
45	$105,000	$106,961,45	$211,961,45
46	$110,000	$119,979,14	$229,979,14
47	$115,000	$134,077,89	$249,077,89
48	$120,000	$149,322,56	$269,322,56
49	$125,000	$165,781,91	$290,781,91
50	$130,000	$183,528,83	$313,528,83
51	$135,000	$202,640,56	$337,640,56
52	$140,000	$223,198,99	$363,198,99
53	$145,000	$245,290,93	$390,290,93
54	$150,000	$269,008,39	$419,008,39
55	$155,000	$294,448,89	$449,448,89
56	$160,000	$321,715,82	$481,715,82
57	$165,000	$350,918,77	$515,918,77
58	$170,000	$382,173,90	$552,173,90
59	$175,000	$415,604,33	$590,604,33
60	$180,000	$451,340,59	$631,340,59
61	$185,000	$489,521,03	$674,521,03
62	$190,000	$530,292,29	$720,292,29
63	$195,000	$573,809,83	$768,809,83
64	$200,000	$620,238,42	$820,238,42

Example 2

Let's say you wait a little longer to invest and you start at age 35 with a goal to retire 30 years later at age 65. You start investing $5000 a year (or $416.67 a month) and have the same average rate of return of 6%. After 30 years, your investment would be worth **$419,008,39**, versus **$151,975,26 (0.09%)** or **$202,842,02 (2%)** if you just put your money in a savings account.

This table illustrates what your annual and total contributions could be as well as what the growth of your money could be over that 30-year time period as a result of compounding.

Age	Total contributions	Rate of return (6%)	Total
35	$ 5000	$ 300	$ 5300,00
36	$ 10,000	$ 918	$ 10,918,00
37	$ 15,000	$ 1873,08	$ 16,873,08
38	$ 20,000	$ 3185,46	$ 23,185,46
39	$ 25,000	$ 4876,59	$ 29,876,59
40	$ 30,000	$ 6969,19	$ 36,969,19
41	$ 35,000	$ 9487,34	$ 44,487,34
42	$ 40,000	$ 12,456,58	$ 52,456,58
43	$ 45,000	$ 15,903,97	$ 60,903,97
44	$ 50,000	$ 19,858,21	$ 69,858,21
45	$ 55,000	$ 24,349,71	$ 79,349,71
46	$ 60,000	$ 29,410,69	$ 89,410,69
47	$ 65,000	$ 35,075,33	$100,075,33
48	$ 70,000	$ 41,379,85	$ 111,379,85
49	$ 75,000	$ 48,362,64	$123,362,64
50	$ 80,000	$ 56,064,40	$136,064,40
51	$ 85,000	$ 64,528,26	$149,528,26
52	$ 90,000	$ 73,799,96	$163,799,96
53	$ 95,000	$ 83,927,96	$ 178,927,96
54	$100,000	$ 94,963,63	$194,963,63
55	$105,000	$106,961,45	$211,961,45
56	$ 110,000	$ 119,979,14	$229,979,14
57	$ 115,000	$ 134,077,89	$ 249,077,89
58	$120,000	$149,322,56	$269,322,56
59	$125,000	$165,781,91	$290,781,91
60	$130,000	$183,528,83	$313,528,83
61	$135,000	$202,640,56	$ 337,640,56

Age	Total contributions	Rate of return (6%)	Total
62	$140,000	$223,198,99	$363,198,99
63	$ 145 000	$245,290,93	$390,290,93
64	$ 150 000	$269,008,39	$419,008,39

Keep in mind that you'd need to factor in the future rate of inflation for more accurate numbers. However, because the average rate of return of 6% that we use in these examples far exceeds today's average rate of inflation, you'd still end up with a pretty nice sum of money regardless. Also keep in mind that in these two examples, the numbers could be significantly higher if you earn a higher average rate of return on your annual investment.

Based on these examples, it's very clear that the power of compounding is magnified the more you invest, the more interest your money earns, and the more time your money is given to grow. So ideally, you want to begin investing as early as you can. Even if you are in your 40s or 50s or beyond, you can still take advantage of the power of compounding over time. In this case, your goal would be to catch up by increasing your investment amounts, which you can do by finding ways to increase your income. For instance, if you invest $10,000 a year ($833.33 a month) with an average rate of return of 6%, you'd have $232,758,77 after 15 years and $548,642,93 after 25 years.

Ensuring You Are Prepared to Invest

For some reason, luck is strongly associated with rich people. One of the assumptions often made about everyday people who become independently wealthy is that they've had some miraculous stroke of luck in life that has brought them financial success. While this might be the case for a few outliers (for instance, recipients of inheritances, windfalls, or lottery winnings), the reality is that the "luck" of most everyday wealthy people comes from their setting specific intentions, having the right mindset, and preparing themselves to pursue and achieve the financial success they desire.

Investing in the stock market is a pathway to wealth building, but it doesn't just happen. Becoming a successful investor requires a level of preparation (and patience) to set yourself up for success in the years to come. So we are going to go over the specific things you need to do to ensure that you are well-prepared to invest.

But first, what happens when you *aren't* well-prepared? Here are a few scenarios I've seen play out time and time again. Folks get excited about investing because they read something or heard something somewhere: a hot tip, a hot stock, the next big thing. The stock market looks great. Everything is on the up-and-up and they need to get on the train fast. They put a chunk of money into an investment, with no goals, no objectives, and no idea of their risk tolerance, and then one of a few things happens:

- Something comes up (a car repair, a girls' trip, a job loss) and they need the money right away – this minute, *now*. And so they sell their investments with minimal or no gains and perhaps they even take on some losses (shoutout to those trading fees).
- After investing, perhaps they see the stock market take a temporary dip a few short weeks or months later. It's all they keep hearing about on the news and in other media, and so panic sets in and they sell their short-lived investments at a major loss.
- Or maybe they're just having trouble sleeping at night because that's a big chunk of cash they invested in the stock market and right about now it feels like one big massive gamble. Plus they have bills to pay, so just like the previous two scenarios, they sell their short-lived investments with minimal to no gains or with big losses.

If you ask me, these are pretty lousy scenarios. Time has been wasted, hard-earned money has been lost, and they're definitely not getting any of those missed hours of sleep back. Fortunately, if you are taking action with this workbook, I know for sure that you are not (or are no longer) about that life. You want to know what you're doing before diving in, and rightfully so.

How exactly should you get prepared before you dive into investing?

Here's a checklist with some key considerations you'll want to keep in mind. If you don't meet all of the following criteria just yet, don't worry or give up on investing. Just add any areas of improvement/next steps to your preparation list so you can set yourself up for success.

Are You Prepared to Invest? A Checklist

	Yes/No	Next steps
You have an income, preferably a steady income. It goes without saying that you need money to invest, even if it's just a little bit. When you're starting small, the key to building your investment portfolio is investing consistently over time. Having a steady income will allow you to make these consistent investments. If you're between jobs or trying to find a job and don't have an income coming in, your focus should first be on making enough money to cover your basic living expenses before you start thinking about investing.	☐	
You're able to meet your financial obligations. While your money is busy working and growing for you in the stock market over the long-term, life goes on in the meantime. That means you still have budgets to create and bills to pay. So before you start investing, you want to make sure you are able to comfortably meet your financial obligations like covering your day-to-day needs and overall living expenses without having to go into debt in order to survive.	☐	

	Yes/No	Next steps
You have emergency savings in place. Your emergency fund is there to ensure that you are able to weather life's storms, like a job loss or other unplanned situations. This fund is essentially a backup plan so you don't have to leverage debt or derail your financial goals when these circumstances arise (which they will, because life happens). Establishing your emergency savings should take priority over investing. Ideally, you want to have three to six months of your basic living expenses put aside before you start dedicating money to investing.	☐	
You have paid off your high-interest debt. Once you have your emergency savings in place, it's time to create a budget and get aggressive with paying down your debt, starting with any high-interest debt you might have. This is important because as we discussed before, interest on debt will compound. Unless you focus on paying off your debt fast (and by that I mean as much as you can possibly afford above the minimum required payment each month), that hole will only keep getting deeper. *An exception: While you are paying down your debt, if your employer offers a retirement plan in which they match your contributions, be sure to contribute enough to get the full match. It's essentially free money and you don't want to leave it on the table. Plus, usually, contributing enough to get the free money comes out to a small percentage that you won't really miss in your paycheck anyway,*	☐	

	Yes/No	Next steps
You have a plan in place for your short-term life changes. Do you have a life change coming up in the near future that will require financial support – for instance, planning a wedding, preparing for a baby, moving to a new city, or leaving a relationship? If yes, it's important that you plan accordingly by making sure you have money put aside to support your life changes. This isn't money that you should be investing because you know you'll need it in the short term.	☐	
You have the right type of insurance in place. Having the right insurance coverage can potentially save you a ton of money in the event of an emergency, an unplanned life occurrence, or a medical need. For instance, the right car insurance can pay for the costs of a car accident, like repairs and medical bills. A homeowner's policy can help you rebuild your home after devastating damage from fire or flooding. Health insurance can pay for expensive emergency room bills after an injury or illness. Disability insurance can protect your income in the event you are unable to work for a period of time.	☐	
You've done your research and have an understanding of what you'll be investing in. Prior to investing, you should spend some time researching your potential investments with a minimum goal of understanding what they are, what they cost, and how they have performed in the past.	☐	

	Yes/No	Next steps
You understand how much risk you can tolerate. As an investor, understanding your risk tolerance can make all the difference in how well you sleep at night. Knowing how much risk you can stomach will in turn help you determine how aggressive or conservative an investor you want to be. Understanding your risk tolerance will also help you eliminate panic when the market is swinging downwards and help you make better buying and selling decisions.	☐	
You have realistic expectations about the long-term performance of the stock market. The average return of the U.S. stock market based on the S&P 500 since its inception in 1926 has been about 10%. Of course, an average doesn't mean it has been 10% every year. There have been years when the average rate of return has been much higher and the stock market has had double-digit gains above 10%. There have also been years where the stock market has had really major declines and, as a result, double-digit losses. But despite the peaks and valleys, over the long term the average return has stayed consistent. While past performance does not predict the future, it's a pretty good benchmark to use, keeping in mind that you'll want to adjust for that 2% average inflation. This adjustment makes the effective historical rate of return between 7% and 8%. So when it comes to setting your expectations, especially as a new investor learning the ropes, I recommend being mentally prepared for the losses as well as the gains.	☐	

	Yes/No	Next steps
You have a plan to diversify your investments. When it comes to investing in the stock market, it's important that you don't go all-in with one type of stock or one industry. Otherwise, you might find that you've taken on a ton of risk when that stock or industry goes through a rough patch. Having a plan to diversify your portfolio also means that you have a plan to mitigate your risk. It's all about having a good mix of investments. This way, even if one stock or industry goes down, the others could keep your overall portfolio stable.	☐	

Setting Your Investment Objectives

As important as it is to plan to invest for the long term, it's equally important to clearly define your investment objectives in relation to your financial goals. Basically, what are the things that you want your money to be able to accomplish for you in the long term? These goals provide two things: your reasons for investing, and how long your investment timeframe is likely to be. Examples of objectives could include things like retiring at a certain age, paying for your child's college education, buying your dream house, creating a family legacy to be passed down through generations, and so forth.

Once you've laid out what your specific investment objectives are, you'll need to:

- Determine how much money you'll need in total for each objective to be met.
- Determine how much you can consistently invest on a recurring basis to help you get closer to achieving your objectives.
- Assign a timeline to your objectives and determine how many years it will take to meet them. (*Tip*: A quick Google search for "investment calculator" will pull up several different calculators to help you determine your numbers.)

Investment objective	Desired total investment amount	Desired year to complete	Number of years to save	Monthly amount
Total monthly amount needed to invest each month:				**$**

As you work on calculating the costs of your objectives, don't worry if the amounts you are able to invest right now aren't enough to meet your objectives within your desired timeline. Consider that you'll likely have more to invest in the future as you pay off debt, increase your income, and reduce your expenses. Make a plan to adjust your objectives over time as your financial situation changes.

Having clear objectives in place, as well as clear timeframes for them, will help you create a sound investing plan and make the best decisions about how and where you invest your money. For example, if one of your objectives is to retire in a particular year, you can plan to make your retirement investments more conservative as you approach that year. By doing this, you ensure that if there is a market decline around the time when you plan to retire, your investments are protected and you can stay on course with your plan.

As a rule, you don't want to invest any money in the stock market that you have allocated for short-term goals that you want to accomplish within five years or fewer. Why? Well, the stock market is hard to predict, so a lot of volatility can happen over the short term. Investing for the long term (the longer, the better) allows you to weather short-term market declines or volatility, because if there is a period of decline, you can patiently wait for the market to recover and grow.

Understanding Risk

When you put your money in the stock market, or in any investment for that matter, you are assuming a certain amount of risk that is unavoidable. Particularly with investing in the stock market, your investments are uninsured and returns are not guaranteed. That sounds scary, but what does it really mean?

Basically, it means that investments can lose their value as a result of company performance, disasters, or other reasons. The stock market can tumble due to economic reasons or political climates. If these scenarios affect stocks you own, then your portfolio could lose value as a result.

However, risk isn't just associated with investing in the stock market. Just about anything you can do with your money carries a degree of risk. For instance, your cash in a savings account is at risk of losing its value over time due to inflation. Buying real estate carries a risk of a property losing value. Opening a business comes with a risk of the business not performing well and having to close its doors. That doesn't mean you should avoid doing these things, either; it just means that when it comes to money, some risk is unavoidable. It's not something to fear, but something you can accept, understand, and work with.

That being said, let's get into some ways in which you can mitigate or hedge against risk.

Mitigating Risk

There will always be a level of risk when it comes to investing, which is basically the possibility that you can lose all or some of your money. This same idea applies to life in general. Life is full of risks, some greater than others. You might be employed at a great company, but you run the risk that you could lose your job if the company has a bad year or the finances are mismanaged. You might purchase a top-of-the-line kitchen appliance, but you run the risk that one day it could just stop working for reasons beyond your control like an electrical circuit overload or a defective part. By making a daily commute to work driving in your car, you run the risk that someone could rear-end you even if you are following all the road rules. The list goes on. In life, people either make sure they do everything possible to minimize their risks (e.g. getting a safe car) or they avoid risk altogether (e.g. not going skydiving).

Given the potential for losses, the idea of risk deters many people from investing. Many consider investing a form of gambling – taking a chance on the unknown and hoping for the best. And they are absolutely correct. Investing is basically gambling, *if* you don't know what you are investing in, have no strategy, and aren't clear on your objectives. However, while risk cannot be completely eliminated from any portfolio, there are ways to minimize it. This means taking specific steps to reduce any adverse effects from external factors that are outside of your control but that can impact the value of your portfolio. It is essentially making sure that you don't put all your eggs in one basket.

So what can you do to minimize risk? Here are three key steps you can take to mitigate your investment risk, in addition to the step you are taking right now, which is getting educated on how investing works:

1. **Get clear on your *why* (i.e. your investment objectives).** For each investment you make, it's important that you are clear on why you are investing and when you'll need your money to meet your objectives. Two questions to ask yourself are:
   - *Question 1: What are you investing for?* Are you investing for retirement? For your kids' college education? For passive portfolio income? For a home several years from now? Knowing what you'll need the money for can guide you toward the type of investments to put your money into.
   - *Question 2: How much time do you have to invest?* If you'll need your money within the next 5–10 years, then it makes the most sense to take a conservative approach to investing. That's because you can't time the market and you'll have less time for your investment to recover and rebound from a loss. Say, for instance, if a recession were to happen 3 years into your 5- to 10-year investment timeline, you might be forced to cash out at a loss because you need the money. If, on the other hand, your objective with a particular investment is to save for retirement 30 years from now, then perhaps you could be a bit more aggressive in the short term, then become more conservative as you approach retirement, because you have more time to ride out any short-term losses.

2. **Determine your risk tolerance.** Once your objectives are in place, knowing your risk tolerance is just as critical. Greater returns come with greater risk, but can you stomach possible sharp declines in the value of your investment during a bad market? It's best to determine what kind of investor you are, be it conservative, aggressive, or in between, so you can avoid the stress and headaches from investing outside of your comfort zone. Also, when you understand what you can tolerate as an investor and you have your objectives in place, you are less likely to be swayed by "hot" stocks or recommendations from people suggesting to get in on an investment "*now!*" (no, thank you).

What kind of investor are you? See which of these three types you relate to the most:

- *Conservative investor:* If your main focus is to keep your initial investment steady and you're fine with less extreme returns, you are a conservative investor. You are okay with very slight dips in the stock market, especially if you don't need your money in the short term. But if you are only investing for the short term, dips in the stock market could keep you up at night. You don't like surprises and you tend to avoid taking big financial risks. As you approach retirement (when it's less than 10 years away), there's nothing wrong with being a cautious investor. However, if you have a longer time horizon, investing too conservatively can mean sacrificing extra earning potential.

- *Assertive investor:* If you have a good sense of risk and understand that the stock market typically always recovers from short-term declines in a matter of time, then you are an in-between or assertive investor. You are comfortable taking more risk in the market and understand market declines could be a great opportunity to get some good investing deals with the proper research. If you still have a while to go (10+ years) before you need your money for an investment objective like retirement, you are okay taking on some additional risk.

- *Aggressive investor:* If you are all about maximizing your earnings in the market and you understand that big earning potential comes with big risk, you are an aggressive investor. You are comfortable with large short-term market dips. You typically don't need your money for 20–30 years and you are all about growing your portfolio as much as possible. As your time horizon shortens, you may change your investments to be more conservative down the line.

3. **Leverage asset allocation and diversification.** There are two key ways to mitigate or balance out the amount of risk you take on.

The first is asset allocation and the second is diversification. These should both be combined to help you create a solid risk mitigation plan. Let's go over what they are:

- *Asset allocation*. This is basically ensuring that you have a mix of different investments in your portfolio (e.g. U.S. stocks and bonds, foreign stocks and bonds, cash, real estate). This way, if one type of investment experiences major losses, the impact to the rest of your portfolio is reduced due to your asset allocation.
- *Diversification*. This, on the other hand, is all about dividing your investments into different categories. For example, by purchasing stocks in different industry sectors like consumer goods, technology, healthcare, energy, telecommunications, and so on, you are creating a well-diversified portfolio. If, for instance, the consumer goods or technology industries experience declines, you still have investments in other industries to balance out your portfolio.

So, What Type of Investor Are You?

Leverage these questions to assess your risk tolerance and determine the type of investor you are. Keep your responses in mind as you research and build out your future investment portfolio.

1. How would you feel if your investment portfolio lost 10% of its value in a month?

   A. Very anxious, I might think about selling my investments.
   B. Concerned, but I'd probably hold onto my investments.
   C. Not worried, I'd see it as a chance to buy more.

2. How long do you plan to invest before you need to withdraw a big chunk of your money?

   A. Less than 5 years
   B. 5–10 years
   C. More than 10 years

3. How do you handle market ups and downs?

   A. I prefer stability and low volatility.
   B. I can tolerate some ups and downs.
   C. I'm comfortable with high volatility for higher returns.

4. What's your main investment goal?

    A. To preserve as much of my capital as possible

    B. For balanced growth and income

    C. For maximum capital growth

If you answered:

- **Mostly A's: You're likely a conservative investor**, prioritizing capital preservation and preferring low-risk, stable returns.

- **Mostly B's: You're probably an assertive investor**, balancing risk and return, and tolerating moderate risk for potential growth.

- **Mostly C's: You're likely an aggressive investor**, comfortable with high risk and volatility for the chance of maximum returns.

Ultimately, your goal with taking these actions to mitigate your investment risk is to keep your risk in line with your comfort levels while maintaining the value of and growing your investment portfolio. Getting prepared to invest will require some groundwork, but it's well worth the time and effort to make sure that you lay the right foundation for your future success as an investor.

CHAPTER **19**

Researching Your Investments

When it comes to stock market investments, there are a variety of different investment types. The reason why it's good to know what types of investments exist (and not just what they are but also how they work) is because this knowledge can help you make the best decisions for your own investment strategies based on your timeline, objectives, and comfort level. So let's get into the most common investment types and how they work.

Investing in Stocks

Stocks, also known as shares, give you an ownership or equity stake in a company. When you buy a company's stock, you essentially become an owner or shareholder. The value of the stock you buy depends on several factors, including the company's size, what's happening in the stock market, the company's potential for short- and long-term growth, and more.

There are two types of stocks you can purchase: common and preferred stock. Both are issued by publicly traded companies (i.e. companies whose stock can be purchased on the stock exchange).

1. **Common stock.** This is also known as ordinary stock. This is the type of stock most people purchase for their investment portfolios. Holders of common stock (shareholders) have certain benefits, like

voting privileges where they can vote to elect a company's board of directors or vote on changes to corporate policy. The number of votes they can make depends on the number of shares they own. In addition, shareholders might receive dividends depending on the company's profitability in a given quarter or year and are provided with the company's annual report, which keeps shareholders informed about the company's performance.

2. **Preferred stock.** Preferred stock has certain advantages over common stock in that preferred stock owners have a greater claim to the company's assets and typically earn a fixed dividend payment regardless of how the company is performing. In addition, if the company goes bankrupt, preferred stockholders get paid before common stockholders. However, preferred stock also has its own disadvantages. For instance, preferred stockholders have very limited or no voting rights. Also, a fixed dividend may actually limit the value of their stocks – for example, if the company is performing much better than the value of the fixed dividend the preferred shareholder is receiving.

Based on the differences between the two types of stocks, you assume more risk as a holder of common stock but stand to gain considerably more than preferred stockholders when the company is doing well and growing.

As mentioned earlier on, companies sell stock to raise capital from investors in order to grow their businesses. You buy their stock and in return they incentivize you by aiming to improve the value of the stock by growing the business. As an added bonus, some companies will even pay out dividends tied to their performance and profitability.

Investing in Bonds

A bond is basically an IOU (I owe you). It is a loan that you as an investor can make to the government, a corporation, or an organization to help them raise money. In exchange, you'll receive earnings based on the interest payments they promise you for the money you loaned them over a specified term. The type of bond issued depends on the entity issuing the bond. With bonds, you face the risk of losing money if the entity in question is unable to pay you back in full or if you cash out your bond investment before the bond term agreement expires. However, bonds are graded by risk, which can help you make smart decisions when it comes to buying them.

What to Know About Bonds

Here are a few terms associated with bonds that are good for you to be familiar with:

- **The borrower or bond issuer.** This is the entity that issues the bond.
- **Interest.** This is the fee the bond issuer pays for what they borrowed. Interest rates can vary across bonds depending on the risk level of the bond, the time until its maturity, and the current market interest rates.
- **Face value.** This is the full amount borrowed.
- **Maturity date.** This is the specific date for eligibility to get the face value back.

Most individual bonds have a face value of $1000. Bond interest payments happen in advance of you receiving your face value back. Just like with stocks, there are also different types of bonds in the United States. They include:

1. **U.S. government bonds.** These are bonds that are sold by the government to help pay down the national debt and for other federal government projects, like infrastructure, and so on. Bonds issued by the federal government are exempt from state and local income taxes and are further broken into two types:
   - **Treasury bonds and Treasury notes.** Treasury bonds pay interest every 6 months and have 30-year maturities, while Treasury notes pay interest every 6 months but have maturity dates of 2–10 years.
   - **U.S. savings bonds.** While U.S. savings bonds don't make regular interest payments, they can be purchased at less than their face value. The advantage to this is that you can get the full face value when you cash them in at their maturity date. So, for example, you can buy a U.S. savings bond for $50 that has a face value of $100. There are also different types of savings bonds: **Series EE bonds**, which offer tax breaks when used for higher education, and **Series I bonds**, which provide protection against inflation by increasing the interest rate as inflation rises.
2. **Municipal bonds.** These are bonds used to fund state and local government projects like building schools, hospitals, and roads in cities. They are typically exempt from federal and state income taxes.
3. **Corporate bonds.** These are bonds issued by companies. They typically pay higher interest rates than government bonds, but they're also higher risk, because if the company goes out of business, it may not be able to pay the interest or face value on the bond. Corporate bonds are also subject to federal and state income taxes.

Investment-grade bonds are seen as stable, less risky bond invest-ments and are typically tied to big corporations or government entities. Junk-grade bonds, on the other hand, are bonds that are seen as high-risk, unstable investments by companies that are having issues keeping up with their liabilities. A brokerage platform with research capabilities will show you bonds by rating when you look them up by their com-pany ticker.

Should You Buy Individual Stocks and/or Bonds?

Now that you have some insight into stocks and bonds as investment types, you should know that you don't have to buy them one by one. You also have the option of effectively buying many stocks or bonds at once by investing in funds.

As we'll go over next, funds provide a simpler way to make sure your money is well-diversified. Buying individual stocks and bonds is often riskier due to less diversification, unless you're individually buy-ing hundreds of different stocks across different company types and industries (which is more labor-intensive and expensive if your broker-age charges a fee per purchase).

If you are new to investing or prefer an easier, more hands-off approach, then investing with built-in variety and diversification is the way to go and starting out with funds is a great idea.

Investing in Funds

Investment funds are pools of money from groups of investors invested in a variety of different stocks and bonds that make up each fund. There are a few different types of funds, including mutual funds, index funds, and exchange-traded funds (ETFs). Let's take a closer look at each one:

- **Managed mutual funds.** A mutual fund is a pool of money from a group of investors set up for the purpose of buying multiple secu-rities like stocks and bonds, all combined into one investment. Mutual funds are typically managed by a fund manager associated with a brokerage firm. Their job is to make investment decisions for the fund and set the fund's objectives, with the main goal of making money for the fund's investors. The active management comes with a price of annual fees that could reduce an investor's overall returns.
- **Index funds.** Index funds are a type of mutual fund, but they are passively managed because they don't need a fund manager

to make active decisions about what stocks to include. By Investopedia's definition, "An index fund is a type of mutual fund with a portfolio constructed to match or track the components of a market index, such as the Standard & Poor's 500 Index." In plain English, this means an index fund can be set up to buy all the same stocks within a specific index (like the S&P 500). So if you were to invest in an index fund tracking the S&P 500, you would be invested in every single one of the 500 companies that make up the S&P 500. You could also purchase a total market index fund, which invests your money in equal ratios across the entire stock market based on a total market index like the Wilshire 5000, which is the broadest stock market index and measures the performance of over 6700 publicly traded companies. A **bond fund** is another type of index fund, which invests in thousands of bonds aggregated into one fund.

- **Exchange-traded funds (ETFs).** ETFs work similarly to index funds and include funds that aggregate stocks or bonds. They are usually passively managed and set up to mimic a particular index. One key difference is that, unlike mutual funds and index funds, which are traded at the end of the day at the market's closing price, ETFs are traded like individual stocks; they can be actively traded throughout the day at whatever the current market price is. For experienced investors trading ETFs, this could be advantageous, as they can track price changes throughout the day and buy or sell ETFs at any point during the day to take advantage of these price changes, which can be pretty substantial. However, with the potential of high short-term gains, there is also high risk involved. ETFs also typically have lower expenses than most mutual funds.[1] However, the fact that they can be actively traded throughout the day means a brokerage may charge commission fees when you buy and sell ETFs, although many brokerage firms in recent times are doing away with these fees.

- **Real estate investment trusts (REITs).** Another type of investment people like to add to their portfolios are REITs. Basically, REITs are companies that invest in real estate. They make investments in income-producing real estate across different sectors like shopping malls and retail spaces, industrial and office buildings, hotels and resorts, technology and data centers, hospitals, storage facilities, farms, and so forth. Many investors like to add REITs to

---

[1]https://www.investopedia.com/articles/investing/102915/why-are-etf-fees-lower-mutual-funds.asp#:~:text=ETFs%20have%20lower%20costs%20on,the%20total%20assets%20under%20management

their portfolios for further diversification and as a way to invest in real estate without having to physically purchase property or deal with property management. Investors in REITs earn a share of the income made from the real estate investments in the form of dividends. Personally, I'm a fan of REIT index funds, which aggregate different types of REITs in different industry sectors like the ones I've just mentioned.

Other key differences between these investment fund types – mutual funds, index funds, and ETFs – revolve around fees and tax efficiencies. ETFs and index funds are almost always cheaper and more tax-efficient than managed mutual funds.

I'd recommend investing in index funds and/or ETFs depending on your investment goals. If you are unsure, an investment advisor can help you to determine your best option. Personally, my favorite way to invest is in index funds. Let's get into why.

Index Funds to Win

Index fund investing is a simplified and extremely popular way to invest that is widely leveraged by people focused on building long-term wealth, because it continues to prove itself as a smart way to invest. Index funds were made popular by Jack Bogle, founder of the investment firm Vanguard, which created the world's first index fund in 1975. Jack Bogle's idea behind creating an index fund was that instead of creating human-managed funds to try to beat the performance of the stock market, index funds could simply track the performance of a benchmark index, which would eliminate more of the potential for human error, incur lower brokerage fees, and in turn realize better returns for investors over time. He proved to be right, even decades later.[2]

Benefits of Index Funds

Index funds are passively managed and as a result are low cost. As I've mentioned, index funds (and ETFs) are set up to mimic specific indices. Because of this, there is no need for them to be actively managed by fund managers or other financial professionals, as there are typically not a lot of changes that happen in the funds' stock or bond

---

[2] https://www.investopedia.com/terms/j/john_bogle.asp

holdings. Some of the most popular index funds have expense ratios as low as 0% to 0.05%, while popular mutual fund expense ratios are much higher and are typically above 0.75% due to their active management.[3] There are even some mutual funds with expense ratios in the 2–3% range. Keep in mind that these expense ratios are charged based on the total amount of money you have invested in your portfolio.

Lower expenses also means larger earnings. You might look at those expense percentages and think, well, it's only 1%. However, the differences in fees can really add up. To put it in real numbers, if you had $10,000 invested in a mutual fund with a 1% expense ratio, you'd be charged $100 in expenses for the year. By contrast, if you had that $10,000 in an index fund with a 0.07% expense ratio, you'd only pay $7. As your portfolio value grows more and more, the differences in expenses stack up as well. Imagine once you have $100,000 invested – it would be painful to pay $1000 in fees that year instead of just $70! Plus, every extra dollar paid in fees is a dollar that can't compound for you over time. So expenses can be a big deal.

Index funds have solid historical returns. Historical data show that when index funds and actively managed funds are compared, index funds perform better over 80% of the time. And this is despite mutual funds and their managers working hard to beat the performance of the stock market indices. In fact, in a report from CNBC, after 10 years, 85% of large-cap mutual funds had underperformed the S&P 500 index, and after 15 years, nearly 92% were trailing the S&P 500 index.[4] Again, this better performance on average translates into better returns for you as an investor. (Also, better performance for lower fees? Sign me up.)

Index funds offer great diversification. Because index funds are made up of hundreds or even thousands of stocks and bonds (often many more than actively managed funds), your investment is very broadly diversified. This diversification helps to reduce your risk, especially during times of market volatility.

Index funds make taxes easier to manage. Whenever securities are bought or sold in the stock market, taxable transactions are created. This happens quite often with actively managed mutual funds. With index funds, trades do not happen as often, which means fewer taxable transactions. If you sell any investments on your own, you'll need to pay taxes on any profits you earned.

---

[3] https://smartasset.com/investing/mutual-fund-expense-ratio
[4] https://www.cnbc.com/2022/03/21/why-index-funds-are-often-a-better-bet-than-active-funds.html

Popular Index Funds

A few examples of popular U.S. index funds from some of the largest brokerage firms include the following:

Vanguard Total Stock Market Index Fund (Symbol: VTSAX)
- This fund is highly diversified and provides investors exposure across the entire U.S. stock market (over 3700 stocks).
- Expenses are 0.04%, that is, $4 for every $10,000 invested (as of 2024).
- Its average annual return since inception in 2001 is 8.20% (as of 2024).

Vanguard 500 Index Fund (Symbol: VFIAX)
- This fund invests in stocks in the S&P 500 Index (a large-cap index).
- It represents 500 of the largest U.S. companies and is considered a good gauge of overall U.S. stock returns.
- Expenses are 0.04%, that is, $4 for every $10,000 invested (as of 2024).
- Its average annual return since inception in 2010 is 7.97% (as of 2024).

Vanguard Real Estate Index Fund (Symbol: VGSLX)
- This fund invests in REITs – companies that purchase office buildings, hotels, and other real estate property.
- Expenses are 0.13%, that is, $13 for every $10,000 invested (as of 2024).
- Its average annual return since inception in 2001 is 8.71% (as of 2024).

Fidelity Zero Total Market Index Fund (Symbol: FZROX)
- This fund is highly diversified and provides investors exposure across the entire U.S. stock market.
- Expenses are 0% (as of 2024).
- Its average annual return since inception in 2018 is 12.43% (as of 2024).

Fidelity S&P 500 Index Fund (Symbol: FXAIX)
- This fund invests in stocks in the S&P 500 Index (large-cap).
- Expenses are 0.015%, that is, $1.15 for every $10,000 invested (as of 2024).
- Its average annual return since inception in 2018 is 10.86% (as of 2024).

Fidelity Real Estate Index Fund (Symbol: FSRNX)
- This fund invests in a variety of REITs across various real estate sectors.
- Expenses are 0.07%, that is, $7 for every $10,000 invested (as of 2024).
- Its average annual return since inception in 2018 is 6.63% (as of 2024).

Schwab Total Stock Market Index Fund (Symbol: SWTSX)

- This fund is highly diversified and provides investors exposure across the entire U.S. stock market.
- Expenses are 0.03%, that is, $3 for every $10,000 invested (as of 2024).
- Its average annual return since inception in 2011 is 7.96% (as of 2024).

Schwab S&P 500 Index Fund (Symbol: SWPPX)

- This fund invests in stocks in the S&P 500 Index (large-cap).
- It represents 500 of the largest U.S. companies and is considered a good gauge of overall U.S. stock returns.
- Expenses are 0.02%, that is, $2 for every $10,000 invested (as of 2024).
- Its average annual return since inception in 1997 is 8.97% (as of 2024).

The main differences between these popular funds are really their expense ratios and the brokerage housing the fund. The average annual fund returns mentioned in the examples are just that: averages. They factor in dips and spikes in the stock markets, recessions, and high-growth years, among other things that drive the performance of the stock market.

Before you put your hard-earned money into any investment, you need to do your research. Essentially, you need to understand what you are investing in and determine whether the investment you're considering has the potential for growth. Doing research, however, can be time-consuming and even overwhelming, especially if you are not sure what to look for or haven't done it before. Fortunately, once you understand what to look for, it gets easier to do. Researching your investment is extremely necessary in my opinion and something I highly recommend, even if you are working with the best investment advisor in the game.

Things to Look for When Researching Investments

Before you decide to make an investment, here are five key things you should be looking for that will help you get a good sense of the level of risk associated with each investment and help you make good investing decisions based on your goals and comfort level:

1. **The company or fund's financial situation and plans.** Any company that issues publicly traded stock is required to issue an annual report to its shareholders. These reports include information

on the company's financial state, such as its balance sheet (details of its assets, liabilities, profits, losses, and available capital); its revenue and expenses; its short- and long-term objectives and plans for growth; its strategy for navigating competition; and more. Funds are also required to provide an annual report to their shareholders that discloses how the fund is being operated, its main goals, and its financial state.

These annual reports are available publicly and can be found on the company or fund's website or with a quick Google search. The U.S. Securities and Exchange Commission website (https://www.sec.gov/edgar/searchedgar/companysearch.html) also allows you to access the annual report filings for pretty much any company that is publicly available. Reviewing a company's or fund's annual report, especially its financials, can help you get a good idea of what the company or fund is about and in turn help you make informed investing decisions.

Some more in-depth factors that you may be interested in if you want to geek out when doing your research for a company's stock would include:

- Whether the company owes more than it owns
- Whether the company is reporting profits, or losses (and why)
- Whether they're earning money from their sales and operations, as opposed to having money coming in mostly due to borrowing activities (aka debt)

All of this information can typically be found in the company's publicly available financial reports.

2. **The company or fund's historical performance.** Looking at historical trends can provide you with important information on how a stock or fund has performed year over year. Essentially, you want to make sure the investment is consistently performing well on average while taking historical economic climates into consideration. For example, the 2008 stock market crash had a hard impact on almost all investments, but some fared better than others. Here are two examples of historical performance charts that are publicly available using an online investment research tool. These two images show the historical performance of Coca-Cola (Symbol: KO) and Vanguard's Total Stock Market Index Fund (Symbol: VTSAX).

The first image presents a high-level snapshot of Coca-Cola's stock (Symbol: KO) since 1970. The dips represent market declines, including the 2008 recession and the 2020 pandemic. A single share of Coca-Cola stock was approximately $0.88 in January 1970, whereas in this snapshot taken in June 2024 it was worth $62.55.

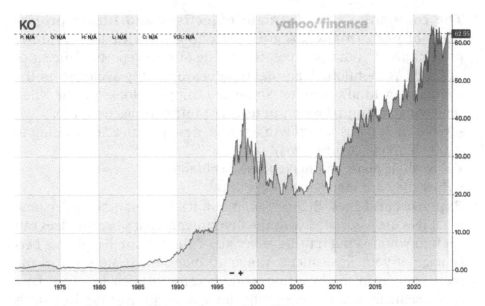

Source: Adapted from https://finance.yahoo.com/chart/KO

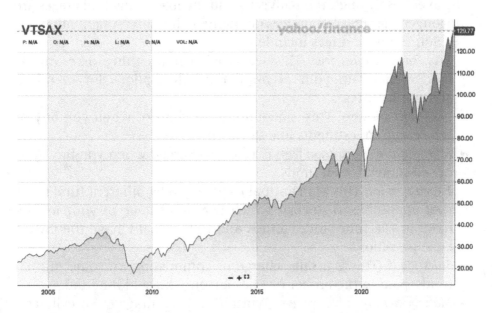

Source: Adapted from https://finance.yahoo.com/chart/VTSAX.

The second image presents a high-level snapshot of the Vanguard Total Stock Market Index Fund (Symbol: VTSAX) since it's been publicly traded starting in 2001. The dips represent market declines, including the 2008 recession and the 2020 pandemic. A single stock of VTSAX was approximately $24 in 2001, whereas in this snapshot taken in June 2024 it was worth $129.77.

3. **The company or fund's main objectives and future projections of performance.** A great place to get a sense for the future projections of your investments is in the annual reports of the stock or fund. As mentioned, annual reports are usually available on the company or fund's website. Some key things to look out for when reviewing an annual report in terms or future projections are:
   - What their plans for growth are (e.g. new products, expanding to new markets, acquisitions)
   - How their plans will make them profitable
   - How they are managing competition
4. **Expenses and fees.** Before you invest, it's important to understand what fees are associated with the investment. That's because fees can eat into your overall returns, especially if the fees are based on a percentage of your investment. Vanguard index funds are some of the most popular in the investing world because of their low fees. Low fees essentially mean more profits for you as an investor. In today's world with high competition among brokerages, and new-age investing avenues through robo-advisors and the like, many brokerages are no longer charging certain fees on many of their investment offerings.
   Some common fees include:
   - *Brokerage account fees.* This fee type includes things like annual fees to maintain your account and subscriptions for premium account features.
   - *Trade commissions.* This is a commission charged when you buy or sell certain investments like stocks or bonds.
   - *Mutual fund transaction fees.* This fee is charged when you buy and/ or sell some mutual funds.
   - *Expense ratios.* This is an annual fee charged by different fund types (not applicable to stocks), which is a percentage of your investment in the fund. Index funds and ETFs usually have the lowest expense ratios.
   - *Sales loads.* This is a sales charge or commission on some mutual funds, paid to the broker or salesperson who sold the fund.
   - *Management or advisory fees.* Typically, a percentage of your investment that is paid to a financial advisor or robo-advisor.
   - *401(k), 403(b), and 459(b) fees.* These are administrative fees to maintain your retirement accounts, often passed on to the plan participants by the employer.
5. **Other considerations (e.g. leadership track records and media mentions).** When you do your research, it can also help to consider things like track records and media mentions. Looking at the track record of a company's CEO or the track record of a mutual fund

manager can provide you with additional insights. A quick Google search or LinkedIn profile visit can tell you about their educational background and investment experience, which is very important given that they are managing millions and even billions of dollars of other people's hard-earned money, yours included. You also want to keep an eye on what's being mentioned in the news when it comes to the company or fund you are interested in, as this could also provide you with valuable insights as you make your investment decisions.

Creating an Investing Strategy

To invest successfully, you need to have a plan of action in place to help you achieve your desired financial outcomes. Having a strategy essentially means creating a roadmap to achieve success with your investments. This applies to how you structure your investment portfolio, how you set up your objectives, and how you determine your timeline. Having a strategy will also help you determine how you buy investments and when you sell them according to your goals and objectives.

There are several different investing strategies out there but personally, I prefer simplified and easy-to-manage investment strategies, specifically, strategies that involve index fund portfolios like the one-fund portfolio, the two-fund portfolio, the three-fund portfolio, the four-fund portfolio, and the five-fund portfolio investing strategies.

These are popular strategies that many investors leverage and love. Let's get into them, starting with the most popular – the three-fund portfolio.

The three-fund portfolio is basically a portfolio that contains three asset types and uses low-cost index funds or ETFs. In the United States, these three asset types are U.S. stocks, U.S. bonds, and international stocks. Jack Bogle, the founder of the Vanguard brokerage firm, was the first to introduce the idea of index fund investing with the first stock index fund. He then later introduced a bond index and international index to provide his investors with more diversification and more variety of asset classes. Based on these three funds, the three-fund investing portfolio was born and made popular by the Bogleheads (bogleheads.org), a forum of investing enthusiasts, named to honor Jack Bogle.[5]

---

[5] https://www.investopedia.com/terms/j/john_bogle.asp

The Vanguard funds that are widely considered best for a three-fund portfolio are:

- Vanguard Total Stock Market Index Fund (VTSAX)
- Vanguard Total International Stock Index Fund (VTIAX)
- Vanguard Total Bond Market Fund (VBTLX)

The three-fund portfolio investing strategy is great for anyone looking for simplicity with investing and a low time commitment. This is because you simply pick three low-cost funds and then align your investments to your investing objectives, rebalancing your portfolio over time as necessary. Among the benefits of the three-fund portfolio are the following:

- **Great diversification.** Due to the variety of asset classes across a three-fund portfolio, there's a high level of diversification, which means a lower level of risk and a high chance of your being able to achieve your investment goals when you leverage this investing strategy.
- **Low cost.** The expense ratios associated with index funds and ETFs are typically the lowest across the various investment types, including actively managed mutual funds. Because the fees are low, you'll have more money to invest and in turn more money that has the opportunity to grow, as opposed to paying high fees, which over time can have a massive effect on the returns in your portfolio.
- **Easy to manage.** Because this strategy has only three funds, it's easy to manage any changes you need to make (e.g. making contributions or withdrawals, updating beneficiaries, tax planning, etc.) and also easy to rebalance your portfolio based on your ideal asset allocation as you achieve your investment goals.
- **No advisor or fund manager risk.** When it comes to this strategy you typically don't need a financial advisor because you're managing your own investments. This means you can save more money and can avoid any conflict-of-interest issues. You can also avoid any issues with fund managers trying to outperform the stock market or making poor investment decisions that you are not aware of.
- **Better than average performance.** History has shown that over the long term, index funds outperform actively managed funds. This is because index funds simply follow index benchmarks to track the performance of the stock market (or a particular sector), whereas actively managed funds are focused on earning higher returns for their investors by outperforming the market, which does not happen often.

Given these benefits, the next thing you probably want to know is how you can go about structuring a three-fund portfolio, or in other words, how you should determine your asset allocation. Well, there are a number of ways to do this.

As mentioned earlier, the three-fund portfolio consists of index funds invested in U.S. stocks, U.S. bonds, and international stocks. If you are early on in your investing journey, you have the opportunity of time to take on more risk and ride out any market downturns and so you might consider a portfolio more heavily weighted in stocks versus bonds. This is because while bonds can be a solid investment, they are typically much more conservative. Where the average return of stocks over the long-term is between 7% and 8%, bonds have typically had an average return of about 3%.

Some examples of how a three-fund portfolio can be structured include:

- Having 80% of your investments in a combination of U.S. and international stocks and the remaining 20% in bonds (this 80–20 approach could be considered aggressive).
- Having your investment equally allocated across U.S. stocks, U.S. bonds, and international stocks, in the amounts of 33% respectively (this equal division approach could be considered as moderately conservative).
- Having 20% of your investments in a combination of U.S. and international stocks and the remaining 80% in bonds (this 20–80 approach could be considered as highly conservative).

Three-fund portfolios are well-suited for new investors. If you'd like to take a deeper dive into the three-fund portfolio, I highly recommend the book *The Bogleheads' Guide to the Three-Fund Portfolio*, by Taylor Larimore.

With every investment strategy, there are always alternatives to consider. The whole idea behind considering other investment approaches is to help you figure out or to confirm which approach will work best for you. So, let's go over a few alternatives to the three-fund portfolio. They include:

- **The one-fund portfolio.** This investing strategy is the simplest of all and involves investing in one single total stock market or broad market fund. This allows you to invest in a diversified mix of stocks across large, medium, and small-cap companies. The idea behind investing in just one fund is that there is a high enough level of diversification across a total market or broad market fund to still minimize risk even though this portfolio may not have a bond investment component to it. Popular total market funds that would work for this model include the following:

- Vanguard Total Stock Market Index Fund (Symbol: VTSAX)
- Vanguard 500 Index Fund (Symbol: VFIAX)
- Fidelity S&P 500 Index Fund (Symbol: FXAIX)
- Fidelity Zero Total Market Index Fund (Symbol: FZROX)
- Schwab Total Stock Market Index Fund (Symbol: SWTSX)
- Schwab S&P 500 Index Fund (Symbol: SWPPX)

- **The two-fund portfolio.** This investing strategy involves investing in a total stock market or broad market fund and a bond fund. If you're looking to add additional diversification and another asset type to your portfolio, you can consider more than a one-fund portfolio. Adding a bond fund to your portfolio can further help reduce your overall portfolio risk. Since bonds are much more stable than stocks, they can stabilize a portfolio during swings in the stock market. Popular bond funds include:

- Vanguard Total Bond Market Index Fund (Symbol: VBTLX)
- Fidelity US Bonds Index Fund (Symbol: FSITX)
- Schwab US Aggregate Bond Index Fund (Symbol: SWAGX)

- **The four-fund portfolio.** This investing strategy involves investing in a total stock market or broad market fund, a bond fund, an international stock fund, and an international bond fund. If you want even more diversification than a three-fund portfolio, this strategy adds an international bond fund. While there are not many international bond funds to speak of, a popular one is the Vanguard Total International Bond Index (Symbol: VTABX).

- **The five-fund portfolio.** This investing strategy involves investing in a total stock market or broad market fund, a bond fund, an international stock fund, an international bond fund, and a REIT fund (Real Estate Investment Trust). Again, this is another way to add even more diversification and additional asset types. As discussed earlier, REITs are real estate investment trusts and the underlying assets in the portfolio are real estate properties – assets outside of the stock and bond markets. REITs are a great way to invest in real estate without having to physically deal with the property or tenant issues. REIT index funds aggregate multiple different kinds of REITs focusing on different property types – for instance, shopping malls and retail spaces, industrial and office buildings, hotels and resorts, technology and data centers, hospitals, storage facilities, and so forth. Some popular REIT funds include:

- Vanguard Real Estate Index Fund (Symbol: VGSLX)
- Fidelity Real Estate Index Fund (Symbol: FSRNX)

(You may also choose to substitute the international bond fund with a REIT fund in the four-fund portfolio strategy).

The ultimate goal when it comes to investing is for your money to grow. As a reminder, you can build these portfolios with either index funds or ETFs. It is common for investors to use ETFs in taxable accounts due to better tax treatment and index funds in tax-deferred retirement accounts.

Below are some popular funds (also mentioned throughout this chapter) that can be used to construct your own investing strategy, whether that's a one-fund, two-fund, three-fund, four-fund, or five-fund portfolio. Use these examples as a foundation to begin researching the best investment approach for yourself based on your objectives.

Keep in mind these are simply examples and it's still very important that you do your research to make sure you understand an investment before you make any decisions (e.g. looking at the fees, historical performance, fund composition, etc.).

Examples of Popular U.S. Stock Funds
- Vanguard Total Stock Market Index Fund (Symbol: VTSAX)
- Vanguard 500 Index Fund (Symbol: VFIAX)
- Fidelity S&P 500 Index Fund (Symbol: FXAIX)
- Fidelity Zero Total Market Index Fund (Symbol: FZROX)
- Schwab Total Stock Market Index Fund (Symbol: SWTSX)
- Schwab S&P 500 Index Fund (Symbol: SWPPX)

Examples of Popular U.S. Bond Funds
- Vanguard Total Bond Market Index Fund (Symbol: VBTLX)
- Fidelity US Bonds Index Fund (Symbol: FSITX)
- Schwab US Aggregate Bond Index Fund (Symbol: SWAGX)

Examples of Popular International Stock Funds
- Vanguard Total International Index Fund (Symbol: VTIAX)
- Fidelity ZERO International Index Fund (Symbol: FZILX)
- Schwab International Index (Symbol: SWISX)

Examples of Popular International Bond Funds
- Vanguard Total International Bond Index (Symbol: VTABX)

Examples of Popular REIT Index Funds
- Vanguard Real Estate Index Fund (Symbol: VGSLX)
- Fidelity Real Estate Index Fund (Symbol: FSRNX)

Start Researching Your Own Investments

1. Head over to finance.google.com, finance.yahoo.com, morningstar
.com, nasdaq.com, or a specific brokerage website, such as vanguard
.com, fidelity.com, schwabfunds.com, and so on. You can pick your
favorite based on visual appeal and ease of use or go with the brokerage firm where you have an account.
2. Under the tools and research section of the site you choose, look up
the index funds mentioned in this section. You can also look up any
other stocks or funds you're interested in to learn more about them
and their historical performance. This is your first step to researching
an investment!

3. Leverage the worksheet below to document your findings.

Individual stocks you are interested in (Enter name and ticker symbol below)	Sector and industry	Today's date	Current price	Purchase fee or commission	Average performance in the last 10 years (%)

Stock/bond funds you are interested in (Enter name and ticker symbol below)	Sector and industry	Today's date	Current price	Expense ratio	Average performance in the last 10 years (%)

CHAPTER 20

Making Your Investments

The foundational aspect of understanding how investing works is extremely important, but the next most important piece is to actually start investing so that everything you've been learning in theory can be put to work in real life and you can start to earn some real money over time.

Other than choosing investments for a workplace plan like a 401(k), the most popular ways to purchase your investments are:

- **Opening up an investment account with a brokerage firm.** With this route you can start investing on your own or with the help of a robo-advisor, which is an online investment service that provides automated, algorithm-based investment portfolio management advice without the use of human financial planners or advisors.
- **Working with a licensed and reputable financial advisor.** This will allow you to get professional guidance on how to invest your money with the option to have them manage your investments on your behalf.

In the following sections, we'll go over what you need to know about each one of these avenues.

Brokerage Firms and Robo-Advisors

When it comes to buying or selling stock market investments, you are going to need a broker (or a brokerage firm) to manage the transaction.

A brokerage firm is a financial institution that manages or facilitates the buying and selling of securities like stocks, bonds, funds, and so on, between buyers and sellers, essentially acting as the "middleman" between both parties. They typically charge commission fees on transactions and can provide you with up-to-date research, market analysis, and pricing information on the various securities you may be interested in purchasing. Examples of large brokerage firms in the United States include companies like Vanguard, Fidelity, Charles Schwab, T-Rowe Price, and TD Ameritrade.

There are three types of brokers that you could leverage to invest in the stock market:

1. **Full-service brokers.** These are basically a one-stop shop for all of your investment needs. They offer money market and brokerage accounts and a wide range of customized financial planning services like estate planning, investment management, and specific individual investing advice via one-on-one sessions with financial advisors, based on your objectives and risk tolerance. As a result of the services they offer, they typically have higher commission fees and other types of service fees (e.g. fees to work with a designated financial advisor), so you need to ensure that whichever full brokerage firm you select is reputable and acts with your best interests as their top priority.

2. **Discount brokers.** Discount brokers offer their services at a considerable discount compared to full-service brokers. Similar to a full-service broker, you can open money market and brokerage accounts with them where you can initiate transactions to buy and sell securities. They are able to offer discounted services because they do not offer customized financial planning advice (i.e. working with a designated financial advisor to develop a plan for your personal situation). However, they do typically have financial advisors available to provide general, nonspecific advice and have human support to help you place investment orders.

3. **Online-only brokers (aka robo-advisors).** Robo-advisors are basically automated online financial advisors that provide financial management services and advice using algorithms and technology without the need of human financial advisors. They provide customized recommendations of diversified investments based on your individual situation and use software to manage your investments without the high cost of a real-life advisor. However, some robo-advisory firms also provide the option to get advice from a human financial advisor at an additional cost. They typically have very low

minimum investment requirements, low fees, regular and automatic portfolio rebalancing, and automated investing, and in many instances they allow you to purchase fractional stocks. Examples of robo-advisors in the United States include companies like Acorns, Betterment, and Wealthfront.

Today it is common to find brokerage firms that provide some or all of these different types of broker services in one place. For instance, many full-service brokers offer discount broker services as well as robo-advisory services. Additionally, many robo-advisory services now offer discount broker services as well. Depending on where you start out, additional broker services might be offered to you as an upsell as your portfolio grows.

Which one should you choose? When starting out with your investment portfolio, you may choose to go with a discount broker or robo-advisor due to the low costs. Particularly for robo-advisors, keep in mind that since their investment recommendations are based on algorithms, they are not financial advisors. This means a robo-advisory firm's algorithm cannot provide you with the level of input that a human financial advisor can provide you if you need to discuss your unique life circumstances or investment objectives. However, as mentioned, some robo-advisory platforms may offer human financial advisory services for an additional cost. Regardless of which service you use, success comes from understanding what you are investing in, being clear about your objectives and risk tolerance, and spending the time to do necessary research to stay on top of your investments.

Leverage this worksheet to narrow down the best brokerage platform for you:

Brokerage platform name	Are there minimums to invest? If yes, what are they?	Are there monthly or annual fees to use their service?	What are the commissions/fees for buying or selling investments?	Is there access to human financial advisors?	How long does it take to access your money after a sale?	Are their online reviews generally positive?

Working with a Financial Advisor

If you decide to work with a financial advisor, it is a decision that should not be taken lightly, because this person is going to be giving you advice and recommendations on financial products and services that can have a major impact on your financial growth over the long term.

Working with a financial advisor can be a great experience, but it's important that you find the right person who understands your needs and whom you can trust and enjoy working with. To ensure you find the right financial advisor for your needs, you can start by asking for recommendations for great advisors from people you know.

You can also do your own independent research by looking up potential candidates on finra.org and on sec.gov; both websites allow you to research the background and experience of financial brokers, advisors, and firms. Once you are comfortable with your findings, you can schedule an initial appointment to get to know the financial advisor and then take an assessment after your meeting to make sure they are someone you would be comfortable working with.

Leverage this worksheet to document key findings of things you'll want to know about a financial advisor during your initial meeting.

Financial advisor's name	Length of time as a financial advisor	Licenses and credentials they hold (Qualifications)	Their compensation structure (Commission/fees)	Their investment philosophy	Their approach to diversification	The brokerage they use as custodian for your investments

Additionally, it may sound like a no-brainer, but you want to ask them, "Are you a fiduciary (someone who is legally obligated to put your client's best interests first)?" This answer should be yes!

Other questions you could ask them could include:

- What type of clients do you specialize in (e.g. retirees, millennials, women, divorcees, etc.)?
- Will I be working with you directly or with your team?
- How often will we meet? What kind of access will I have to you?

Even if you choose to work with a financial advisor, it's important that you still have an overall financial plan that you are working with (i.e. a plan to pay off debt, save for emergencies, goals, etc.). It's also still a good idea to educate yourself about your investments, because no one cares about your finances more than you do.

CHAPTER **21**

Investing
for Retirement

For most of us, the task of saving for retirement falls entirely on us. Most of us don't have a pension plan, and Social Security (in the United States) is probably not going to provide us with enough money to live anywhere close to a comfortable lifestyle. When it's time to retire, there's no one waiting for us with a mansion on the beach, millions of dollars in the bank, and a bottle of champagne, who's going to say, "Hey, girl! While you were living your best life, I was doing all of this just for you!" Seriously, it doesn't matter how much wishful thinking we do, it's just not going to happen. So taking matters into your own hands to save money and invest for retirement is critical.

You may want to retire early to travel more and spend more time with your family. You could do a "partial retirement" where you opt to work part-time or only when you feel like it. Or you may not be interested in retiring until your later years. Regardless of what retirement scenario you'd prefer, the bottom line is that you're going to need money to live out that ideal and comfortable life in retirement. Personally, I imagine my retirement being fun and stress-free, spending time with my family, traveling at leisure, and living my best life – and I know that "best life" is going to cost me money!

Types of Retirement Investment Accounts

When it comes to investing for retirement, there are different account types you could have, each with their own benefits and drawbacks. They include the following:

- **401(k) – Employer-sponsored.** A 401(k) is an employer-sponsored retirement savings account that only an employer is allowed to offer. Contributing to this account type allows employees to save and invest for retirement on a tax-deferred basis. This means you don't pay income tax on your contributions until you start making withdrawals from your account at retirement.

- **403(b), 457(b) – Employer-sponsored.** Similar to the 401(k), the 403(b) is specific to employees of public schools, certain tax-exempt organizations, and certain ministers, while the 457(b) is specific to governmental and certain nongovernmental employers and their employees.

Benefits and Drawbacks of the 401(k), 403(b), and 457(b):

Benefits
- Many employers will match your contributions up to a certain amount. Matching is a program that some employers offer to encourage you to invest in your retirement with them. When you contribute to their employer-sponsored retirement savings plan, they will match that amount, up to a certain limit, for free. Basically, they are giving you free money for investing in their plan.
- Contributions grow tax-deferred, which means you won't have to pay taxes until you start making withdrawals when you retire. These contributions also lower your annual taxable income during your working years.
- These account types allow for extra catch-up contributions if you are above the age of 50.

Drawbacks
- There's an annual limit on how much you can contribute (however, employer contributions don't count toward this).
- You'll have to pay taxes on your money when you retire.
- There are stiff penalties for early withdrawals under the age of 59½.
- These account types typically have fewer investing choices than IRAs.

- **Roth 401(k) – Employer-sponsored.** In addition to the 401(k), many employers offer a Roth 401(k) option to their employees, which allows you to make contributions with your after-tax income. It works the same way a Roth IRA does (see overview below), but the main difference is the contribution maximum is much higher, similar to the traditional 401(k).

- **Traditional IRA.** A traditional IRA is an individual retirement account that allows you to make contributions with your pre-tax income up to a specified amount each year. Come retirement, you will have to pay taxes on any withdrawals you make on the account, just like with a 401(k). An IRA can be set up independently or offered by your employer.

Benefits and Drawbacks of the Traditional IRA:

Benefits
- Contributions grow tax-deferred, which means you won't have to pay taxes until you start making withdrawals when you retire. These contributions also lower your annual taxable income during your working years.
- You can open an IRA regardless of your employment situation, as long as you've earned taxable income that equals or exceeds your contribution amount for the year.
- This account type allows for catch-up contributions if you are above the age of 50.

Drawbacks
- IRA contribution limits are much lower than the 401(k), 403(b), and 457(b) plans.
- You'll have to pay taxes on your money when you retire.
- There are stiff penalties for early withdrawals under the age of 59½.

- **Roth IRA.** A Roth IRA is an individual retirement account that allows you to make contributions with your after-tax income up to a specified amount each year. Come retirement, your withdrawals will be tax-free, including all profits you've earned. A Roth IRA can be set up independently or offered by your employer.

Benefits and Drawbacks of the Roth IRA:

Benefits

- Your contributions are made post-tax (i.e. after taxes have been paid on your income), which means there is no deferred tax benefit, but the earnings on your contributions will not be taxed come retirement age.
- You can make withdrawals on your contributions (just not your profits) before you are eligible without any tax penalties.
- You can open a Roth IRA regardless of your employment situation, as long as you've earned taxable income that equals or exceeds your contribution amount for the year.

Drawbacks

- There are income limits determining who is eligible to contribute.
- IRA contributions limits are much lower than the 401(k), 403(b), and 457(b) plans.

- **Simplified Employee Pension (SEP, or SEP IRA): Employer and self-employed retirement plan.** This retirement plan is most commonly used by small businesses and those who are self-employed (with or without employees), and allows you to contribute up to 25% of your earnings up to a certain amount, tax-deferred. Only employers (including yourself as a self-employed sole proprietor) can make SEP contributions, and each eligible employee (including yourself) must receive the same contribution percentage from you as the employer. A brokerage firm can typically help you set up this account type.

Benefits and Drawbacks of the SEP:

Benefits

- You have the flexibility to choose your contribution requirement depending on how your business is doing, and contributions are not required each year.
- Contributions grow tax-deferred, which means you won't have to pay taxes until you start making withdrawals when you retire. These contributions also lower your annual taxable income during your working years.
- Contributions are deductible on your business tax returns.

Drawbacks
- There are stiff penalties for early withdrawals under the age of 59½.
- You cannot make catch-up contributions if you are above the age of 50.

- **Solo 401(k) or one-participant 401(k) – Self-employed retirement plan.** This retirement plan is specific to those who are self-employed but have no full-time employees (with the exception of a spouse). It offers many of the same benefits of a traditional 401(k), but with a solo 401(k), business owners can make contributions both as an employee and as an employer, which allows them to maximize both their retirement contributions and their business deductions. This plan also covers spouses who get an income from the business. A brokerage firm can typically help you set up this account type.

Benefits and Drawbacks of the Solo 401(k):

Benefits
- A solo 401(k) is a great way to contribute for retirement as a self-employed person, because you can contribute more than what is allowable in an IRA.
- You have the choice of selecting a traditional solo 401(k), where you make pre-tax contributions, or a Roth solo 401(k), where you make post-tax contributions.
- You can take loans from your solo 401(k) if needed, although I wouldn't recommend it.
- This account type allows for catch-up contributions if you are above the age of 50.

Drawbacks
- You cannot contribute to this plan if you have full-time employees.
- You cannot contribute to this plan if you are already contributing to a 401(k) with an employer – for example, if you have a side hustle where you are self-employed but are also still working full-time and contributing to an employer's plan.

▶ **Note**

You can find out more about the various retirement account types, eligibility, and contribution limits on the IRS website (IRS.gov).

- **Non-retirement accounts.** These are accounts that you can set up independent of any employer. You can save for retirement in non-retirement accounts by leveraging a brokerage account where you invest your after-tax money. While non-retirement accounts do not have the tax benefits of retirement accounts, you'll still be saving money. Because you've already paid taxes on your deposits when you make them, you'll only be required to pay taxes on your earnings when you sell assets at a profit (capital gains), and there are no withdrawal penalties. So, while you don't benefit from the tax shelter, you also don't have to wait until age 59½ to take out your money.

Now that you know more about the different types of retirement accounts, you can decide which is right for you. Like the sound of more than one? It's possible to have a combination of these different retirement avenues, depending on your eligibility. You can find out about your eligibility on the IRS website (IRS.gov).

What to Do When You Leave Your Employer

In today's working world, most people no longer stay at their jobs for their entire working careers. As a matter of fact, according to a survey done on Baby Boomers by the Bureau of Labor Statistics, the average worker has had 12.3 different jobs between the ages of 18 and 52, and that number is only expected to keep growing for Millennials and Gen Z.[1] Each time you switch jobs, it's quite common to contribute to a new retirement plan as well. When you're leaving an employer whose plan you have contributed to, you want to ensure that you take your money with you when you leave so you can continue saving effectively for retirement. This is called a rollover.

When you leave a job, you can roll over your money in your former employer's plan into an independently established rollover IRA at a brokerage firm of your choosing. The nice thing about having the money in your own IRA is that you can then invest more cost-effectively with much lower fees and with more transparency than your former employer's plan may have had. Moving your retirement savings into an account outside of your former employer will give you access to the entire stock market. Plus, many employers charge maintenance fees for

---

[1] https://www.bls.gov/opub/ted/2019/baby-boomers-born-from-1957-to-1964-held-an-average-of-12-point-3-jobs-from-ages-18-to-52.htm

maintaining former employees' accounts, and these fees can add up, so you definitely don't want to leave your money there.

What about rolling your money over into your new employer's plan? Many companies will allow you to do a retirement plan rollover, where you can move your retirement savings from your former employer's plan into the new employer's plan. However, if you are changing jobs, it's better to move your retirement savings into your own IRA account with a brokerage where you have access to the entire stock market and potentially much lower fees as opposed to moving your money into your new employer's plan.

It's important to keep in mind that transferring the funds into a non-retirement investment account will be considered an early withdrawal and those distributions, if made from pre-tax accounts, will be subject to income taxes and an early-withdrawal penalty. Be sure to review the IRS website (IRS.gov) for qualification requirements and specifics on rules, restrictions, penalties, and exemptions. Transferring it to another retirement account – such as a 401(k) to an IRA, or a Roth 401(k) to a Roth IRA – is your best bet for a simple rollover.

Tips to Maximize Your Retirement Investments

As you invest for retirement, here are some key steps you should consider taking to ensure you have the nest egg of your dreams:

- **Take full advantage of your employer's match if they offer one.** If your employer offers a match, take full advantage of it by contributing enough to get the full match. Otherwise you'll be leaving free money on the table, and nothing beats free money.
- **Start contributing toward your retirement savings as soon as you can.** Time is your best friend when it comes to building long-term wealth, especially for retirement. Thanks to the power of compounding, the sooner you start, the more money you'll have come retirement. Starting later? You'll need to be willing to play some catch-up and make the extra effort by saving and investing more. This might mean stepping outside of your comfort zone by getting a better-paying job, adding a part-time job, or starting a side hustle to increase your income.
- **Max out your contributions if possible.** Not only will maxing out your annual contributions give you an annual tax break – because contributions to traditional plans are pre-tax, such as 401(k), 403(b), 457(b), and traditional IRA – but it will also get you

closer to your retirement savings goals. If you are unable to max out your contributions right away, that's okay. Start with small increments of a percentage or two every quarter or every six months.

- **Diversify your retirement investments.** It's all about choosing a mix of investments that can help you maximize your returns while still mitigating risk. Don't put all your money into one stock (including your company stock!), since doing this greatly amplifies your risk.
- **Roll over your investments when you leave your employer if you participate in their plan.** If you're switching jobs, it's better to move your retirement savings into your own IRA with a brokerage firm. This way you have more investment options and can avoid high fees.
- **Don't borrow or withdraw from your retirement savings.** Does your employer give you the option to borrow from your retirement savings account? While this may sound like a great option, don't get too excited yet; when you look at it closely, it might not be such a great idea. Withdrawing or borrowing money from your retirement savings can have adverse effects on your wealth-building efforts over the long term for a number of reasons:
  - Like many people who borrow from their retirement accounts, you might have to reduce or stop your new contribution amounts altogether in order to be able to make the loan repayments.
  - You will lose the potential long-term gains/earnings you would get if your money had remained invested and was working for you.
  - You will lose out on the effects of compounding when you take money out of your retirement savings accounts.
  - If you quit or get fired while you have a loan pending from your retirement account, you will have to repay it in full almost immediately; otherwise you will have to pay an early withdrawal penalty.
  - If you withdraw your money before your eligible retirement age (e.g. cashing out when you leave a company or from an IRA), you will be liable to pay income taxes as well as an additional 10% penalty on the total amount withdrawn.
  - If you are making a withdrawal from a nontaxable retirement account like a Roth IRA, you will still be liable for income tax on your earnings as well as a possible penalty based on the total amount withdrawn (although you can withdraw the amount you've contributed without penalty).

What does this look like in actual numbers? Let's say that right now you are considering taking $1000 out of your pre-tax retirement account as a withdrawal (e.g. from a traditional IRA). Let's also assume that the average return on your investment for the next year would be about 8%. At the end of that year, you'd have $1080 in your account. In another year after that, based on annual compounding with a return of 8%, you'd have $1166 from an original investment of $1000.

However, if you decided to take that $1000 as an early withdrawal instead of leaving it to grow, you'd have to pay the following (assuming a 30% tax rate):

Early withdrawal penalty of 10% = −$100
Federal and state tax withholding = −$300

As a result, the balance you receive would only be $600.00. In addition, your original $1000 would miss out on the potential earnings and compounding over the years to come, so the lost opportunity is even greater.

It could be that you are eligible to take a loan from a 401(k) that you will pay back over time. While you won't be subject to paying a penalty or taxes in this scenario as long as you pay back the loan, it is likely that you'll be paying interest on the loan amount in addition to (again) sacrificing potential earnings and compounding.

However, if you left that money alone for 10 years, the potential future value of your $1000 retirement savings could be $2159, assuming an average return of 8% over that 10 years. That's $600 versus $2159. The difference is major. And this is only based on our example of $1000. If it was based on $10,000, it would be a difference of getting $6000 immediately versus $21,590 in 10 years. I'll just leave that right there.

Are You Saving Enough?

As you save for retirement, another important thing to consider is whether you are saving enough. Basically, how much do you need to live comfortably during your retirement years, given that retirement can last on average upwards of 20–25 years? Here's how to determine your number.

Step 1: Determine how much you'd need on a monthly basis to live comfortably in retirement. This monthly amount should include things like your living expenses, travel, fun, and so on. Basically, add up the cost of all the things – your essentials plus fun – that you'd like to be able to afford for a full life when you are retired. Take the monthly amount you've decided on and multiply it by 12 so you know how much you need each year.

For example, let's say you decide you'll need $4000 a month. $4000 multiplied by 12 months comes out to $48,000 a year that you'll need to live comfortably, assuming this number is after taxes. Multiplied again by 20 years ($48,000 × 20), again assuming the average length of retirement (starting at 65), you'll need to save $960,000 for your retirement. In order to make sure you are factoring in taxes, you'll want to add on a tax rate of at least 25% to this so you can cover your annual tax obligations when you start to make withdrawals. This would bring the amount you'd need to save to $1.2 million before taxes. Keep in mind that your annual tax rate will depend on how much you withdraw as income from your retirement account on an annual basis.

Formula:

1. *Monthly living expenses in retirement × 12 months = Annual living expenses*

_____ *× 12 =* _____

2. *(Annual living expenses × 20 years average retirement) × 25% (tax obligations) = How much to aim to save for retirement*

(_____ *× 20) × 25 / 100 =* _____

Step 2: Project what you are currently saving for retirement now into the future to determine how much you'll have. How much are you able to save now? Do you anticipate that increasing in the future? You'll also want to figure out how much you *should* be saving on an annual basis to ensure you meet your long-term retirement goal. Your calculations will need to factor in inflation, and you can play around with seeing how potential investment returns could speed up your journey. A good online retirement calculator can help with both of those things. Keep in mind that you may decide not to retire completely and instead have a part-time job or business. So, in addition to investments, consider that you may have additional income coming in from a job or business.

Looking at things this way can help you understand how much you need to save to live the life you desire. The good news is that you don't have to save every single spare dollar you have for retirement and sacrifice living a good life right now. You just need to contribute consistently to your retirement account and invest your contributions accordingly. Investing over time will allow your money to compound and gain returns in the form of growth and dividends, which means your money is at work and growing; you just need to give it time.

Investing During Retirement

While we frequently talk about retiring by a certain age, it's important to keep in mind that retirement is not a specific date or moment in time; it's a period of time that can last for decades. That means when you retire, you won't be withdrawing all your money at once, so your money still has more time to keep growing. You should also be spending less in retirement than you did while working. Ideally, any expenses related to your kids are gone or greatly reduced (e.g. childrearing and educational expenses), and your mortgage might be paid off. So your taxable withdrawals and in turn your taxable rate should be lower.

Withdrawal rate. Speaking of withdrawals, one way to plan how much to take out from your investments in retirement is by determining your withdrawal rate. Your withdrawal rate is the percentage of your portfolio that can be withdrawn per year, to ensure that you don't run short of money during your retirement years. A simple formula that is commonly discussed to help figure out your withdrawal rate is the 4% rule. According to Investopedia,[2] this rule seeks to provide a steady income stream to a retiree while also maintaining an account balance that keeps income flowing through retirement. The 4% withdrawal rate is considered to be a sweet spot, as the withdrawals will consist primarily of interest and dividends. For example, if you know you can comfortably live on $40,000 a year in retirement, then your goal would be to save $1 million for retirement so that as you withdraw 4% on an annual basis, your account balance will remain relatively steady as your investments continue to make money and you'll have enough to last your entire retirement.

In retirement, you also still want to ensure that you have an investment strategy in place that transitions to making your investments more conservative as you age. This will help you hedge against major losses in a market decline and keep your mind at peace about your finances while you enjoy your retirement.

---

[2] https://www.investopedia.com/terms/s/safe-withdrawal-rate-swr-method .asp#:~:text=The%204%25%20rule%20states%20that,limiting%20how%20 much%20is%20withdrawn

Leverage this checklist to make sure you are on track to save for retirement:

☐	**Determine how much you need to save for retirement and set your annual retirement account contribution goals based on the IRS maximum contribution limits.**
☐	**Determine if your employer offers an employer-sponsored retirement account and if there is a match.** If they do not offer a retirement account, you can open up a traditional and/or ROTH IRA, independent of your employer.
☐	**Do your research and choose your investments.** Alternatively, you can select a target date fund, based on your investment objective of when you intend to retire. A target date fund automatically adjusts your asset allocation to become more conservative as your retirement date approaches.
☐	**Start contributing to your retirement savings each pay check.** At a minimum, contribute enough to get your employer match if one exists. If no match exists, consider contributing some of your income to take advantage of the pre-tax benefits (e.g. 5–10%).
☐	**If you are not already maxing out your contributions, determine how you can increase your tax-deferred retirement contributions with a goal of maxing out.** If you are unable to max out at this time, start with small percentage increments every quarter or every six months.

When it comes to taxes, be sure to consult with a tax professional if you need specific guidance. Also be sure to confirm the latest tax rates on irs.gov.

CHAPTER **22**

Checking In on Your Investments

Rebalancing your portfolio is all about checking in on your investments periodically to ensure your asset allocations are in line with your objectives and you are comfortable with the performance of your investments. It's important to keep in mind that rebalancing your portfolio should be part of your long-term investing strategy. Investing requires patience and as you practice patience over the long term, you might find your portfolio going through short-term swings and declines that periodic rebalancing can help you minimize.

As you consider rebalancing, remember that you are investing for the long-term and patience is a key factor for your investing success.

How Does Rebalancing Work?

Let's say you have $100,000 invested in the stock market and your current objectives involve keeping 70% of your portfolio in stock funds and 30% in bond funds. You've chosen this investment split because you are looking to achieve growth with your stocks and mitigate risk with your bonds. This equals a portfolio with $70,000 in stocks and $30,000 in bonds. Let's then say that over time, the value of your stock investments doubles and they are now valued at $140,000, and your bonds are valued at $40,000. Your portfolio is no longer balanced according to your objective, since your stock investments now make up 78% of your portfolio instead of 70%. If your objective remains the same, you'd need to rebalance your portfolio by selling some stocks (−$14,000) and buying more bonds (+$14,000) to get you back to that 70/30 split. However, if your objectives have changed, and you instead are taking a more aggressive approach to your investing and want a larger percentage of stocks in your portfolio, then there's no action required on your part. This is a simple example of how you could approach rebalancing your portfolio.

When to Rebalance Your Portfolio

To elaborate even further, you may want to consider rebalancing your portfolio if any of the following happens:

- **Major gains or major losses significantly change your asset allocation.** You'd need to determine how much money you want to have in one asset class, industry, or investment type as you invest. Based on this determination, if major gains or losses occur that change your asset allocation, then that could be a good time to rebalance your portfolio.
- **Your financial goals and objectives change.** Perhaps you decide to move your retirement date up 10 years earlier or move it out 10 years later. You might decide you want to invest for your child's college education or do more socially conscious investing. Scenarios like this might require that you adjust your portfolio accordingly to accommodate these changes to your goals.
- **You are approaching retirement.** As you approach your big retirement goal, it's typically recommended that you get more conservative with your investments so that if the market goes through a decline, your portfolio and in turn your life plans are not heavily impacted.

How Often Should You Rebalance Your Portfolio?

So how often is too often when it comes to rebalancing your portfolio? A good baseline is to review your asset allocations and rebalance your portfolio, if needed, once a year. Rebalancing your portfolio unnecessarily or more than once a year might be excessive if the changes in your portfolio are minimal. It can also get expensive and eat into your returns due to any associated transaction fees and taxes on earnings when you sell your stock market investments.

Target-Date Funds, Robo-Advisors, and Portfolio Rebalancing

One easy way to get around rebalancing your portfolio on your own is by investing in a target-date fund. A target-date retirement fund is an age-based fund designed to gradually shift your asset allocation over time to fewer stocks and more bonds and cash, so that the fund becomes more conservative the closer you get to your retirement year, minimizing your investment risk over time. If you are invested in a target-date retirement fund, you typically don't have to worry about rebalancing your portfolio, as this is done automatically in the fund each year as you move closer to retirement. However, it's important to keep in mind that target funds are typically actively managed by a fund manager and this means potentially higher fees, which can eat into your investment returns.

Another easy way to get around rebalancing your portfolio is if you have your investments with a robo-advisor that includes the benefit of automatic portfolio rebalancing based on the objectives you specify when you set up your account. You will be able to adjust your objectives as needed and the robo-advisor service will use your selections for future portfolio rebalancing as necessary.

With target-date funds and robo-advisors, you want to make sure you monitor your accounts periodically to ensure your investments are performing in line with your long-term goals.

Letting Go of a Losing Investment

Sometimes as investors it's easy to get super-vested in a company because we love their products or services so much, we are going off the company's past glory, or perhaps we just really love the company's founders. However, sometimes we need to let go of certain investments that might be holding our portfolios down.

But how do you know when it's time to give up and take a loss on an investment that's losing you money? Well, it could be that the investment hits your sell point price – the minimum price at which you'd sell to avoid further losses. It could also be that the company's fundamentals have changed for the worse, the company is continuously embroiled in scandal, or the industry or market segment is declining beyond your comfort level.

In the end, it's important to remember that selling an investment at a loss is not the end of the world and surely if you keep investing, you will more than make up the difference with big winners in the long run. You can't say that will happen in a game of poker!

Staying on Top of Your Investments

☐	**Set a calendar reminder to review your investment portfolio every quarter to ensure your investments are performing in line with your long-term objectives.**
☐	**Next, set a reminder to rebalance your portfolio once a year.** If necessary, sell the investments that are putting your asset allocation off balance and then buy more of what you need to attain the right balance. If you use a robo-advisor and have it set to auto-rebalance, check in on any changes. Working with a financial advisor? Bring up rebalancing your portfolio at your check-in meetings. **Note: Nothing to rebalance?** That's perfectly fine. If your portfolio remains in line with your current objectives, then you don't need to change anything. It's not necessary to rebalance your portfolio just for the sake of rebalancing – this can get expensive.
☐	**Not sure you want to do this on your own? Plan to schedule time to speak with a financial advisor who can help you.**

PART III

Side Hustles

CHAPTER **23**

Preparing for a
Side Hustle

Preparing to build a *successful* side hustle starts with establishing the right mindset. Yup! We are back to mindset.

From setting financial goals to budgeting to paying off debt to saving and investing to – you guessed it – starting a side hustle, having the right mindset is foundational and critical to your success at each stage.

Having the right side hustle mindset gets you ready for the journey ahead, and nurturing your mindset along the way keeps you motivated and focused. This in turn increases your chances of success. But why is mindset so important when you are starting or growing a side hustle? After all, isn't a *side* hustle something you just do on the side?

Well, it depends on how you choose to view your side hustle. Yes, by definition a side hustle is something you do on the side, before or after your primary job. It's a side activity in your spare time that can bring in some extra income (the money potential is what distinguishes it from a hobby). Simple, right? However, depending on what you do and how you do it, your side hustle can open the doors to so much more.

A side hustle gives you the opportunity to increase your income *and* create multiple streams of income. Your side hustle can accelerate your journey to becoming debt-free, meeting your savings and investing goals, supporting your family, and building generational wealth.

There are also many instances of well-executed side hustles that generate enough revenue to replace the income from the owner's full-time job, giving them the option to be *their own* boss on *their own* schedule if they decide to do so. Essentially, your side hustle can create a multitude of options for your life, and those options equal freedom and the ability to follow your passions! How about that for something you just do "on the side"?

If deep down you believe your side hustle has the potential for incredible success and you are not willing to put a limit on how far it can go, then you are setting the stage for endless potential and incredible success (even if you don't know how you'll get there just yet).

Like I said, your mindset will keep you motivated and focused, and this is important because starting any kind of business is hard. Even "just" a side hustle takes hard work, time spent away from doing things with your loved ones, early mornings and late nights, learning new things, and testing, testing, and testing again.

All of that being said, preparation for success is vital to get you ready to face these challenges. This means preparing your mindset, figuring out your schedule, adjusting your lifestyle (if only for a season), and establishing a way to stay accountable as you work on your side hustle.

Adjusting Your Schedule with Intention

By adjusting your schedule to accommodate working on your business, you are being intentional about putting your desire for success into action. It's you designating a set period of your days, weeks, and months to put in the effort and making time for your success.

You can adjust your schedule so you wake up early to work on your business before you go to your main job, or you may decide to stay up late after your house has quieted down. You can dedicate time to your side hustle on the weekend. Whatever schedule you settle on, set reminders (e.g. phone alarms or computer notifications), and create a prioritized daily to-do list. Intentional actions like this will enable you to build consistency around the actions you need to take to build your side hustle.

▶ **Tip**

Make your calendar updates and reminders fun! This will motivate you each time you look at your schedule and get those reminder alerts. Just seeing your calendar show "Work on my amazing business!" from 5 a.m. to 7 a.m., or getting a reminder like "Hey, Queen! It's time for XYZ task; you got this!" can be just what you need in that moment to make things happen. You could even cue Rhianna's "Work" song (♪ *work, work, work, work, work* ♪) as your "It's time to work" alarm. Who said this journey couldn't be fun?

Juggling Your Side Hustle and Your Full-Time Job

Once you get into the flow of building your business, things can get really exciting. But if you are also employed full-time, you have only a limited amount of time each day between work and your other responsibilities. You may find that as your side hustle efforts start ramping up and consuming more of your time and energy, it can impact your focus and quality of work at your full-time job.

If you find yourself using your side hustle as an excuse for diminishing performance at work, that's a red flag. After all, you likely still rely on your full-time job to cover your bills and sustain your lifestyle while you get your side hustle off the ground. It's important to make sure you are meeting (and even exceeding) expectations to avoid being called out or even let go for performance reasons, which could put you in a bad financial situation.

When you get to the point where your side hustle is pulling in the big bucks, you can decide to work part-time or leave your full-time job altogether. In the meantime, you want to ensure that you're minimizing any negative impacts to your job while you still need it to pay the bills.

This means prioritizing your to-do lists and creating a schedule where you dedicate focused time to work on your side hustle and focused time to meet your work obligations. If you work nine to five, don't borrow time from your work schedule to brainstorm about your side hustle (except on your breaks or other downtime).

Finding more time in the rest of your day could mean spending less time on your favorite hobbies, waking up earlier, going to bed later than normal, meal-prepping easy foods to cut down time spent on cooking, and so on. You'll probably have to make sacrifices, but remembering your "why" will help you stay motivated for the season in which you have to do this.

Developing the Personal Characteristics You Need for Success

Your journey to a successful side hustle is unique to you and what you ultimately want to accomplish. That said, there are four characteristics that I see over and over in the most successful entrepreneurs:

- **Patience**, because great things need time
- **Focus**, because distraction deters from success

- **Perseverance**, because you'll need to manage your emotions, make sacrifices, and keep going when it's hard
- **The right mindset**, because all those dreams and goals you'll accomplish start first in your head and in your heart

These characteristics are core to your success, so keep them in mind as you work on your business.

That said, let's talk through what you imagine your side hustle to be, what you can learn from any previous experiences you've had, and then lay out how you can best manage your time to build a successful side hustle.

> Think big. Write down what you imagine your side hustle could become. You don't need to have all the answers of how you'll get there or have all the money to make it happen right now; you just need to know that you *can* get there.

If you currently own or have attempted a side hustle in the past, now is a great time to reflect on your experience. (Never had a side hustle? Skip the next three questions):

What went well and what didn't? Why?

What are the key lessons you learned from the business experiences you've had?

How do you imagine yourself doing things differently this next go around?

Now it's time to make time to succeed!

How much time can you realistically dedicate to your side hustle each day/week?

Based on your previous response, how can you lay out your current schedule to ensure you make time to work on your business and take action each day, no matter how small?

What distractions can you minimize or eliminate during your side hustle time?

Whom can you ask for support or accountability to stay on track?

CHAPTER **24**

Laying Out Your Business Idea

One of the most common comments I hear from aspiring business owners is "I want to start a side hustle but I'm not sure what to start," or "I want to grow my business but I'm all out of ideas." Well, every great business starts and grows with ideas, so now we are going to talk about brainstorming your business ideas to help inspire you on your journey.

You've probably had a ton of different business ideas pass through your mind over the years. If you've ever seen a product or service and thought to yourself, "I had that idea first!" well, so have I! There are so many things I see every now and then that I know I definitely thought about as an idea, even if it was for a fleeting moment. (Excuse me while I shed a tear for all the times I could have been a billionaire if only I had pursued the idea. . .*sigh.*)

As human beings, what typically happens when an idea comes to mind is:

- We embrace it and decide to pursue it.
- We decide we aren't passionate enough about it to pursue it.
- We almost immediately come up with excuses as to why we can't do it and quickly dismiss it before we even give it a chance. *It's too hard, someone else is already doing it, it's too complicated, I don't have the right skill set, I don't have time,* and so on.

The truth is, ideas come a dime a dozen, and the only ones that really count are the ones you actually pay attention to, pursue, and try out. This means that if we never made the effort to pursue an idea, we can't

187

cry over what we didn't accomplish because we didn't do anything in the first place. (Excuse me again while I check myself for those wasted tears I just shed!)

Ideas can come to you randomly, like having an *aha* moment on how to solve a problem you constantly face but could never find a good solution for. They can come to you in the shower or while you are exercising – two scenarios when you have fewer distractions so your mind has a greater opportunity to get creative. Your ideas can come to you from thinking about the talents and passions you have, or from someone else bringing a problem or opportunity to your attention, or from sitting down for an intentional brainstorming session.

I can relate to all of the above. In my case, my best ideas come to me in the shower when I'm belting it out loud, completely out of tune, and feeling super-relaxed. (*Ding! Ding! Ding!* That's how the name "Clever Girl Finance" came about, from my girlfriends telling me, "Hey, girl, you should try out XYZ," and from making time for those aforementioned intentional brainstorming sessions.)

One thing to keep in mind is that your business ideas don't *have* to be tied to your passions. Yes, in many instances, this is the case, and it's great to pursue your passions – but it's also perfectly fine to start a business if it's tied to your skillset or past experiences or if you simply have an interest in it. What's even more important than passion is commitment: having the determination and follow-through to do what it takes to make your business successful.

Once you've put yourself in the mental space where you are ready to start or scale your side hustle, start listening to your flashes of inspiration. Anytime a random idea comes to you, write it down. Even if you don't act on it right away, writing it down will put it on your list of contenders that you can revisit and explore in more detail later on. No matter how long it takes you to get back to these ideas, writing them down is key. I've forgotten so many ideas I've had simply because I didn't write them down. So now I make sure that whenever an idea comes to me, I write it down, and when I revisit it later, I'm always glad I made a note of it.

Examples of Business Ideas and Popular Niches

Since we are on the topic of ideas, here are some examples of business ideas that can be executed regardless of the industry or niche you are focused on:

- Create and sell physical products or services (e.g. by starting an ecommerce website or opening a brick-and-mortar store).

- Create and sell digital products online (e.g. books, guides, courses, etc.).
- Coach, teach, or consult for a fee based on a skill set or expertise you have (credentials may be required depending on the field).
- Become an affiliate for a reputable product or service and get commissions on sales you refer (no pyramid schemes, please!).

In addition, some of the most popular niches to start a side hustle include:

- Health and wellness (e.g. fitness, nutrition)
- Food and beverage (e.g. baking, catering)
- Technology services (e.g. website development, graphic design)
- Beauty and style (e.g. skincare, makeup, hair products, fashion)
- Personal improvement and education (e.g. coaching, consulting, teaching, speaking)

Niches that are typically recession-proof during economic downturns, especially when focused on staples rather than optional luxuries, include:

- Technology and IT
- Food and beverage
- Health services
- Legal services
- Financial services
- Repair or maintenance services
- Baby essentials
- Childcare services

Do you already have some ideas churning in your mind? If so and you are feeling inspired, pause here and get to brainstorming! Taking action when you're feeling most inspired is a great way to keep your momentum going. In fact let's do that right now.

Write down your ideas. What current business ideas do you have? Write them down here regardless of what they are. This way you don't forget them, and you can revisit in the future even if you decide not to pursue them right away.

No ideas yet? Do a brainstorming session! Take some time to do some intentional brainstorming on any business ideas you come up with. Feel free to repeat your brainstorming sessions until you settle on a business idea you want to pursue. Don't dismiss any of your ideas until you've got a chance to think them through.

Establishing Your Business Vision and Mission

Once you've got your ideas in place, two really important pieces of building a successful business are your business vision and mission, both of which should align with your values and what's meaningful to you as an individual. So let's get clear on what each one really means.

The *Oxford English Dictionary* defines vision as "the ability to think about or plan the future with imagination and wisdom."[1] Establishing your vision is essentially determining what dreams and goals you ultimately want to achieve and laying out a plan to accomplish them without placing any limitations on your potential. This idea of establishing a vision can be applied to any aspect of your life, including your side hustle. For example, our vision statement at Clever Girl Finance is: "Empower women to pursue and achieve their dreams of financial wellness in order to live life on their own terms."

Your business *mission* is similar to your business vision, but it focuses on what you want to accomplish today and in the immediate short-term time frame ahead of you – for instance, the next one to five years. It is based on your overall business objective and your approach to reaching that objective. Your business mission translates into your mission statement, which is typically a short sentence that encapsulates your objective. You'll often see mission statements on the "about us" pages of business websites. Using Clever Girl Finance as an example again, our mission statement is: "Provide the right education, products, and services for women to become financially successful, minimizing the impact of any socioeconomic barriers limiting them."

It's not uncommon to see vision and mission statements that are blended together or extremely similar to each other, especially in large companies, but you'll find that these blended statements encompass both their current and future goals and objectives.

But why should having a business vision and mission even matter to you if you're just building a side hustle? Well, regardless of the type of business you are building and no matter how small you are starting out, having a defined vision and mission is essentially your business "why." And as mentioned earlier, having a "why" is what will keep you focused and motivated to ultimately achieve your goals. Side hustle or not, it's a good idea to have both a long-term vision and a current mission for your business.

---

[1] https://www.oxfordlearnersdictionaries.com/definition/american_english/vision

Craft Your Business Vision Statement

To get clear about your business vision, think long-term, focusing on success, and on the big dreams you imagine coming true for your business. Don't worry about what you don't know yet; you'll figure it out along the way. Focus on thinking big!

Craft Your Mission Statement

To craft your mission statement, think about your immediate business objectives, including whom your business is for, how it will positively impact your customers and/or your community, and how you intend to accomplish those objectives.

Keep in Mind

- As your side hustle evolves, and as you learn and grow, you may change these statements to stay in line with your goals and values, and that is perfectly fine. It's also perfectly fine for these statements to be short and sweet.
- Stay ambitious. Dream big and don't limit your vision. Leverage your immediate mission to create an actionable approach to achieving your ultimate vision.
- Keep your personal values in mind. Ultimately, whatever business you create, you want it to be in line with your values as an individual, which in turn will keep you excited to work on it.

CHAPTER **25**

Beginning Your
Business Plan

So let's talk about the beginnings of your business plan! Yup, even with a side hustle, it's important to have a strategy in place for your business, and that's what your business plan is all about. Whether your business is brand new or tenured, having a laid-out plan will provide you with a roadmap of actionable steps. By creating this plan, you'll get to really assess your business idea and determine what you want to ultimately accomplish. It's an important step, because going through the process of creating a business plan can potentially help you avoid making costly mistakes with your hard-earned money.

Having a business plan is also essential if you need to pivot or make adjustments in the way you plan to run your business or with the products and services you offer. In this scenario, you'd be able to easily look at your existing strategy and take an objective assessment of where you need to make changes.

If you are navigating a busy full-time job, family, and/or other life obligations, the idea of creating a business plan might feel daunting. Business plans typically have lots of pages full of tons of information, so creating one could very easily become a huge time suck. Due to the popular (yet misleading) idea that a business plan has to be an incredibly lengthy document, a lot of business owners make the mistake of creating a business plan just for the sake of creating one, packing it full of irrelevant information never to be reviewed again.

Why do people do this? Often, they feel that in order to create a good business plan, it only makes sense to mimic a big, successful company. So they do a Google search and end up finding a publicly

195

available business plan from a massive company with thousands of products, services, and employees, and use this large company's plan as the template to craft their own. What typically happens with this approach is that the business owner ends up getting extremely frustrated and overwhelmed – #throwthewholebusinessplanaway – and may give up before they even give their business a chance because they got permanently stuck in this planning phase. The exercise ends up being a complete (and unnecessary) waste of precious time.

At the early stages of a business, leveraging the plan of a massive company that has been around for decades is more confusing than it is helpful, simply because your business is at a completely different stage. Your business plan does not need to be a thousand-page document. Nor does it need to be a hundred-page document. It can simply be a few pages that map out the details of your business in a way that makes sense to you. Consider your business plan an ongoing work in progress that helps you map out your path as you work on your business. You can adjust that path as necessary as you change or improve your products and services, learn more about your audience, and grow your business. It's essentially your business blueprint that you revisit often to ensure you are on the right path with your long-term business goals.

What to Include in Your Business Plan

So, with all of that being said, what exactly should you have in your business plan? Well, as I mentioned, you want to create a plan that makes sense to you and that you can easily review. Whether it's long or short (totally up to you), here are some key things you should consider including in your plan and some questions to consider that can help during the process.

- **What your business is about.** Just as it sounds, this is essentially you outlining exactly what your business does. This would be the place where you include your business vision and mission statement (which we went over earlier). To get clear on this section, start by answering this question: "What pain point does my target audience have, and how do I intend to solve it with this business?"
- **What your legal entity will be.** You'll also want to ensure that your business is set up correctly, both legally and tax-wise. This is where the structure of your business comes into play. Is your business going to be a sole proprietorship, partnership, limited liability company (LLC), or perhaps even a corporation? At the very minimum, you should consider getting it incorporated into an LLC due to the liability protection. As you think through what the best legal structure is for your business needs, two invaluable resources to

guide you on your entrepreneurial journey are the business and taxation sections of your state government website (visit IRS.gov and search "state government websites") and the U.S. Small Business Administration website (sba.gov). These resources go into specific detail regarding the business structures mentioned in this section. They also include the pros and cons of each, as well as the specific steps you need to take to set up your business under any of these structures.

- **Whom your business is for.** Whom do you imagine being your ideal customer on a recurring basis? You'll want to identify who they are, including things like where they're located, their age, their income, and why they would be interested in your business.
- **The products and/or services you plan to offer.** What products and services do you plan on offering? Are they in line with the problem your business will be solving? It's also a good idea to start thinking about how you will price your products or services in this section.
- **Your competition/what already exists.** No business plan is complete without some rough ideas about your competition. Where is your competition located? What are the strengths and weaknesses of their offering? And of course, how can you differentiate yourself from them and make your offering better? The more you understand your competition and what exists in your space, the better positioned you are to find opportunities to make your business stand out from the crowd.
- **Your plan to promote your business.** How and where will you be selling your products and services? How do you intend to engage and attract your ideal customer? This will tie into how you leverage social media, your website, your brand, and other avenues to effectively generate sales.
- **Your business finances.** Having a firm handle on your business finances is key to building a successful and profitable business. Have you identified what your startup costs will be? What about your monthly recurring expenses? How much would you need to earn at a minimum each month to break even and then become profitable? These are all business finance questions you want to start thinking about.
- **Your business goals.** The same way you have goals for your personal life, you should set goals for your business. Basically, what do you want to get done, and by when? Be sure to include revenue goals and break your goals down weekly, monthly, quarterly, and annually. Don't overwhelm yourself with too many things to do at once. Instead, stick to three to five main goals and add on as you accomplish them.

- **How you will manage your business.** How much time can you dedicate each day toward working on your business? What will your schedule look like? What help will you need? It's important to determine how much time you can dedicate to growing your business and the kind of help you think you'll need (social media management, packing and shipping, customer outreach, etc.). This will help you set clear objectives and deadlines around what you need to get done.

Laying out all of these pieces will help set the foundation for a solid business plan and strategy that can guide you and give you clarity around making your business decisions. Remember that it's not about how long your document is; it's about creating a useful plan to help you build the business you desire!

▶ Don't Forget Your Federal Employer Identification Number

As you set up your business structure, one additional thing to think about is obtaining your Federal Employer Identification Number (EIN). This is your business tax ID that the IRS may require you to have, depending on the business structure you've selected. Your EIN is essentially like your Social Security number but is specifically for your business. It ties into your business tax filings, hiring employees, and other important and required legalities for your business.

Obtaining an EIN can be done through a completely free service offered by the IRS (so beware of anyone trying to charge you for it!). Just visit IRS .gov and search "How to apply for an EIN." It's a very straightforward process and all you need to do is follow the instructions.

How to Get Clear on Your Ideal Customer

When it comes to identifying your ideal customer, creating a "customer avatar" can be extremely helpful. **Your customer avatar is basically a detailed profile that represents the person whom you'd want to buy your products and services.** It's the person you are trying to get to know, so you can create products and services that serve their needs and solve their specific problems with a positive outcome. Think of creating a customer avatar like starting a new relationship with someone you want to get to know really well.

As you lay out your customer avatar, some things you may want to include are things like their age, gender, marital status, education level, whether they have children, their occupation, income, and location. You could also want to outline their likes and dislikes, where they hang out, what their main pain points are (life, family, work, etc.), and exactly how your business can solve those pain points.

To narrow things down even further, you can ask yourself questions like:

- "What is my ideal customer trying to accomplish by leveraging my products and services?"
- "Where are they currently getting the information to solve their problems?"
- "What existing brands or companies do they trust?"
- "Why would my business be attractive to them?"
- "What would make them *not* want to purchase from me?"

Depending on your type of business, you can have more than one customer avatar. Keep in mind, though, that the whole idea behind creating these avatars is to ensure that you know exactly whom you are trying to reach and you are creating the right products, services, and marketing strategies to reach and help them. Creating too many avatars can be confusing and cause you to lose focus because you are spreading your efforts too thin. Starting with one or two avatars is ideal to give you maximum clarity about your plan to reach your ideal customers.

Keep in mind that as you lay out your avatars, it's okay if you make some assumptions to start. As you learn more about your target audience, you can fine-tune your avatars. In addition, as your products and services evolve and as your business grows, your avatars may change. It's all about ensuring that you continue to speak to your ideal customer; if your ideal customer changes over time, so will your avatars.

Defining Your Products and Services

Getting clear on your products and services will help you properly describe what it is you are selling and in turn fine-tune the way you communicate to your customer about your ability to meet their needs, encouraging them to buy from you. You'll develop your marketing approach based on two things: whom you help and what your business offers.

Start by laying out the specific products and services you'll be selling. What exactly are they? I recommend simply starting out with one or two products or services, instead of offering many all at once. Starting small will give you the opportunity to really focus on your initial offering, test it out on your audience, make adjustments, and ensure that you have the right product–market fit (i.e. the right products or services that satisfy your ideal customers' needs). Once you've accomplished this with your first few products, you can expand your offerings to leverage the new insights you've gained. If your test is unsuccessful, you can quickly move on to the next product or service you want to test with your ideal customer – again, leveraging the valuable insights you've gained.

Having too many products or services right away can be confusing to manage and make measuring their individual successes and outcomes difficult. Especially when you consider everything else that goes into running your business, you don't want to overwhelm yourself.

As you think through your products and services, you want to keep in mind that whatever your offerings are, they should add value and meet your customers' needs. For example, if you sell books, your customers are buying your books for the knowledge or entertainment they contain, not just for the sake of physically owning a book. (After all, knowledge is why you picked up this particular book, right?) If you sell fitness coaching, your customers are really buying health, not just a workout session. It's easy to get caught up in product ideas and come up with a long list of products and services that you think your customer will like. However, you need to make sure those product ideas align with their pain points, needs, or wants, and also align with what you want your business to be about.

Once you have your products and services laid out, you'll also want to figure out what variations of each specific product or service you'll offer, how you'll price them (we'll be covering pricing your products in the business finances section of this book), and how you'll deliver them. It's also worth considering what forms of payment you'd accept and what return policy or guarantees you'd offer.

With all of this planned out, you can now create your first product or service description, highlighting the value it offers and how exactly your offering will meet your customer's needs. This description will go on your website and will be tied to your social media and marketing efforts.

Remember, as you gain new insights, you can edit and adjust all of this as you feel necessary.

How to Assess Your Competition

When it comes to your competition, even gaining a little bit of insight into how they operate can help you with some key decision-making. Keep in mind, your goal with assessing your competition is to learn from them and gain insights to help you grow your own business. Here are some key steps to help you get started with your assessment:

- **Determine who your competitors are.** When it comes to assessing your competition, the first step is obviously to determine who they are. Specifically, who your *direct* competition is. These are the businesses that currently exist in your space and offer similar products and services that meet your ideal customers' needs. Usually, your direct competitors will be a similar size or slightly larger than your business. Create a list of these competitors as you identify them so you can do a deeper analysis on them later. A top-five list is a great baseline of competitors to start with. As your business grows, this list may change.

- **Take a look at the types of products and services your competitors sell.** This will help you gain insights about what they offer and in what variations. You'll also learn about their pricing structure and how they offer discounts, which can help you assess the quality of their products and services in relation to their pricing. Keep in mind that price is just one of the many reasons that customers choose to buy a product. It all boils down to how valuable they find the product, which could be based on a combination of different factors, including branding and brand perception, the purchase experience, and product quality, among other factors.

- **Understand how they market and sell their products and services.** Looking at your competitors' marketing and sales strategies can help you gain a better understanding of how they acquire their customers. This means understanding the channels they use for marketing and selling, whether they're promoting their business through a blog; via social media platforms like Instagram, Facebook, and Pinterest; by making videos on YouTube; through word-of-mouth referrals in their community; or a combination of all of the above. You also want to know where they have their strongest marketing presence across all the various platforms.

- **Review their customer experience.** Another great way to assess your competition is to take a look at what their customers are saying. While reviews on the actual competitors' websites are a good start, businesses will typically curate their best reviews to showcase on their own websites (I mean, who wouldn't!). However, by reading the comments on their social posts, searching their popular hashtags, or reading what customers are saying about them on various online forums, you may be able to get a more realistic glimpse of what their average customer experience is like. You can even take your research further and make a purchase to get a sense of the end-to-end experience for yourself as well. A customer's experience is extremely important to your business because a great experience can make them raving evangelists for your business (yes to free marketing!) and a poor experience can cause them to deter other potential customers from buying from you. So when it comes to your competitors' customer experience, take note of what people are loving, and what they are not.

- **Determine their strengths, weaknesses, and potential opportunities.** As you go through each of the already mentioned assessment steps, also take note of what your competition does really well (their strengths), what they don't do well or could do better (their weaknesses), and based on this, what opportunities exist for you to differentiate yourself or fill an existing gap. This helps you determine how to better position your business for success.

Lastly, if you're worried about harming other small businesses by competing with them, put those fears to rest. When it comes to competition, there's enough room for everyone to succeed, because ultimately you bring the uniqueness of you to what you do, and no one can replicate that. They'll attract some customers with their specialties, and you'll attract others who prefer what you're offering.

Also note that while it's definitely worthwhile to understand your competitors and how they operate, going overboard can sidetrack you from your goals. Your main focus should be on what *you* ultimately want to accomplish for your business. Keeping an eye on your competition is just one more way to enhance your learning and motivate your success.

Create the First Part of Your Business Plan

This first part of building your business plan comprises:

- Initial to-do's
- What your business is about
- What your legal entity will be
- Whom your business is for
- The products and/or services you plan to offer
- Your competition/what already exists

Use this section to create your business plan to make sure it serves your current needs and helps you accomplish your business vision. Feel free to move your plan to a spreadsheet or document file.

Note: If you don't have all the answers right away, fill out what you know and come back to it when you do. Remember, this is a work in progress.

Initial To-Do's

☐	Take some time to decide on a business structure that will work best for your type of business, paying specific attention to liability protection. (I'd definitely recommend an LLC or that you eventually convert to an LLC once you get your business up and running.)
☐	Be sure to leverage the resources provided in the business and taxation sections of your state government website (visit IRS.gov and search "state government websites") and the US Small Business Administration website (sba.gov). They offer excellent insights and guidance for most questions business owners have.
☐	Apply for your Federal Employer Identification Number if you haven't already by going to IRS.gov and searching "How to apply for an EIN."

What your business is about:

What your legal entity will be:

WHOM YOUR BUSINESS IS FOR (Your Avatars):

Age range:

Gender(s) you are targeting:

Marital status:

Education level:

Do they have children?

Occupation:

Income range:

Location:

Their likes and dislikes:

Where they hang out:

Their main pain points in relation to your business:

Exactly how your business can solve their pain points:

What is your ideal customer trying to accomplish by leveraging your products and services?

Where are they currently getting the information to solve their problems?

What existing brands or companies do they trust?

Why would your business be attractive to them?

What would make them *not* want to purchase from you?

YOUR PRODUCTS AND SERVICES

What exactly are your products and services?

What variations of each specific product or service will you offer?

How will you price each product and service?

What payments will you accept?

What return policy or guarantees will you offer?

YOUR COMPETITION:

What similarly-sized businesses currently exist in your space that have similar products and services that could meet your ideal customer's needs?

What products and services do your competitors offer, and at what price?

How would you describe the value of their product?

How do they market their products and services, and on what platforms do they have the strongest presence?

What are the main sales channels they leverage?

What is their customer experience like?

Overall, what would you say are your competitors' strengths and weaknesses, and what potential opportunities can you take advantage of to help your business stand out?

The upcoming sections will cover the following aspects that also tie into laying out your business plan.

- Your plan to promote your business
- Your business finances and goals
- How you will manage your business

CHAPTER 26

Branding and Marketing Your Business

Branding and marketing your side hustle are key to getting noticed and building a loyal customer base. And that's what we'll be covering next in this workbook as the next part of your business plan, starting with your brand.

Defining Your Brand

Branding is an incredibly important part of a business. It is essentially the look and feel of your business, and it ties directly into the way your potential customers perceive your business. This perception includes what they think about your online presence, your storefront, and the actual products and services you have to offer. And this perception is also important for building likeability and trust.

Branding is much more than just having a nice logo. So many people assume that once you have a nice logo, your branding is set, but a logo is just a small part of your overall brand. With so many businesses, products, and services competing for your potential customers' attention, your brand can be your key differentiator among your competition.

Developing the look and feel for your brand means creating a brand identity that ties into your business vision and mission. It includes your business name, logo, color palette, and typography/fonts. These pieces can then be leveraged to convey your brand identity through your website, storefront, social media presence, product packaging, customer emails, business cards, and more.

When you have a strong brand identity, people easily recognize your business and know what to expect from you (quality and a great experience), and it becomes easier to reach and connect with your target audience. Plus, a strong brand identity can help validate your pricing so you are not perpetually selling at a discount – which is what happens to so many businesses that are overwhelmed by their competition but don't have a strong differentiator to carry them through.

So let's get into some of the key pieces you need to craft a compelling look and feel for your brand.

The Name of Your Business

Your business name is likely to be one of the very first things people will remember about your business. And so, when it comes to naming your business, you want to make sure it's easy to remember, easy to pronounce, and easy to spell. Essentially, if I went to search for your business name on Instagram or Google, it should be a no-brainer for me without the additional exercise of trying to figure out how it's spelled, if it has multiple underscores or periods between letters, or any other likely confusing nuances. Simplicity is key, because the harder it is for people to find you, the more likely they are to give up and move on to the next business – and you don't want that!

Your Business Logo

I mentioned earlier that your business logo isn't your *entire* brand identity, but it is the face of your business and will be your brand identifier on everything from your website to your social platforms to your marketing materials to your product packaging. As a result, you want to create a logo that is beautiful, stands out, and is easily recognizable.

There are so many incredible free online tools and resources to help you create a stunning logo. Websites like canva.com, wix.com, shopify.com, and more all offer logo design options. You can also hire a graphic designer on platforms like etsy.com, upwork.com, or fiverr.com to help you come up with some logo options. Keep in mind that as your business grows and evolves, so can your logo.

Colors and Fonts

You can consider your brand colors and fonts as the building blocks of your brand identity. Let's discuss each one.

- **Brand colors.** Color is a great way to convey your brand identity, especially because colors can have different meanings and effects on your ideal customer. This meaning and effect can impact whether or not a person will be attracted to your business offerings, which is why it's a good idea to understand the basics of color psychology as you select a color palette for your business. Color psychology is basically how colors impact psychology, behavior, and emotions. You can learn more about color insights at colorpsychology.org. As you choose a color theme for your brand, you can leverage a combination of shades, tones, and accents to mix things up. Be mindful of overusing any one single color or too many colors, as this can be overwhelming. Pinterest is great for pulling together color inspiration as you work on crafting your brand identity.

- **Brand fonts.** The fonts you use to convey your brand messaging are also known as your brand typography. As a general rule of thumb, you want your fonts to be easy on the eye and approachable. The last thing you want is for someone to click off from your website because the fonts were too small, too close together, or just generally hard to read. The two basic font types are serif and sans serif fonts, and https://fonts.google.com and https://fonts.adobe.com are great places to browse for font ideas.

Take some time out to name your business, design your logo, and decide on your colors and fonts. Make a note of them below for reference.

My business name: _____

Logo design location: _____

Brand colors; note the Hexadecimal (Hex) and RGB colors:

_____

_____

Brand fonts:

_____

_____

Your Brand Story

Stories are extremely powerful – they're a major way humans forge connections and relate to one another. **Your brand story is essentially the narrative of your business that can help you connect with your ideal customers.** It showcases how and why you started your business, and what your purpose is. It is an essential add-on to your website's "about" page – the same place featuring your business vision and mission statement. It can also be woven throughout your content and marketing strategy to drive customer engagement.

A compelling brand story makes you memorable, establishes trust, and ties into your customers' overall experience with your business by allowing you to create an emotional connection and bond with them that goes beyond a mere financial transaction.

In this day and age, customers want to connect with brands on a deeper level than just fancy packaging. They want to connect with brands that not only solve their problems and meet their needs but also align with their values and make them feel prioritized. If done right, your brand story can create loyal customers and raving fans, which in turn will directly impact the growth of your business.

Having a brand story is not just important for building lasting relationships with your customers; it's also important for anyone who works with you, whether they are partners, contractors, or employees. Your story impacts the culture and operations of your business and helps anyone who works with you to understand your business purpose and the potential impact they can make in your business and the lives of your customers. It can also serve as a form of motivation for you, as you run and grow your business.

That being said, let's talk about how to craft your own compelling brand story.

Crafting Your Brand Story

As you start to think about your brand story, reflect on the experiences that brought you to this point. You'll want to craft an authentic narrative that represents you and your business. Here are some key tips:

- **Start with your mission statement.** Earlier, we discussed creating a mission statement, and this is a great foundation on which to build your brand story. Since your mission statement highlights your business objectives, whom your business is for, and how it positively impacts your customers and/or your community, you can use it to identify the values you want your brand story to convey.

- **Take a deep dive into the details of why you started your business.** This is where you can really tell the story of your brand without having to stick to one or two sentences. Write down how you had the initial flash of inspiration to start your business, what compelled you to start it, and what you were experiencing. Talk about how you've gotten to where you are today and why you believe in what your business offers. Include any interesting facts that can help establish a bond with your customers.

- **Know your audience.** As you craft your brand story, remember that you are not writing it for yourself. You are writing it for that ideal customer you want to attract. Think about your customer avatars you built earlier, and write as if you're speaking to that person to develop the tone and style for your story. It's usually a good idea to showcase your personality, passion, and even humor in your brand story so it doesn't feel generic or cookie-cutter. This will help your business stand out and make your brand more relatable.

Jot down the first draft of your brand story with help from the tips in this section.

- Start with your mission statement and build your story from there. Include your business vision and values.
- Lean into the details of why you started your business. Don't be shy. This is your opportunity to really express your *why* and the meaningfulness of what you do.
- Create a story that speaks to and engages your ideal customers. They will be the ones reading it. You want to pull them in and really connect with them in your narrative.

As with other parts of your business, your brand story will evolve and change as your business grows.

Your Online Presence and Content Strategy

In today's world, it's almost impossible to have a business without having some sort of online presence, whether that's your own website or social media accounts on one or more platforms. It's now second nature for people to do a quick Google or Instagram hashtag search to learn more about a business, read reviews, or find contact information. In addition to having an online presence, creating consistent and relevant content is more important than ever in order to stay top-of-mind with your ideal customers. Given the fast pace of social media, you want to stand out among the many distractions competing for their attention. When it comes time for your ideal customer to purchase a product or service that you offer, you want them to think of you first, and consistent content creation can help to make that happen. It reminds them of your business's name and what you do, along with a touch of personality.

Having an online presence is a foundational aspect for any business because it can be such an incredible marketing tool. In my opinion, creating your own website should be your first step to establishing your online presence, because this is essentially your home base and a platform you own. You pay for your domain name, you pay for your website hosting, you own it.

When you really think about it (and you read the crazy fine-print agreements that we knowingly or unknowingly agree to. . .*yikes*), you may have a presence and build a following on the many social platforms that exist today, but neither the platform nor the following you build actually belongs to you; they belong to the platform in question. This means that if Instagram, TikTok, or Facebook shut down today, your presence on those platforms and the audience you've built there would go away, and you have no control over that. If these platforms decide to make changes to their algorithms, limiting who can see your updates (which they do all the time. . .*argh!*), there's also absolutely nothing you can do about it.

With your website, on the other hand, unless you intentionally shut it down, or your domain or hosting subscription lapses, you have complete control over your site and the content you share there.

Time and time again, I see business owners who are based solely on social media and don't have a website. Their businesses (and thereby their revenue) are directly impacted by the constant algorithm changes the various social platforms make. Even if they have a large following on these platforms, new algorithms can mean each post is reaching a smaller and smaller audience unless the business is paying for ads – because those social platforms are looking to make money, too.

As a result of not having a website, these businesses are missing out on the opportunity to attract new audiences via Google and other search engines. Also, no matter what type of business you have, having a website is a way of establishing credibility. There are many times I've found a company on Instagram, searched for their website, found nothing, and because of this, did not make a purchase.

In addition to the points I've just made, when you have your own website, you can also better showcase your products and services, provide clear access to customer service (this is a big one – ever seen the angry comments people leave on social media when they don't have access to the customer service contact for a business?!), and share updates and content that might be too lengthy or detailed for the fast pace of social media.

With all of that being said, let's get into how you can establish (or improve) your online presence and create a content strategy to engage with your ideal customers and stay top-of-mind when it's time to buy.

Establishing Your Online Presence

As mentioned earlier, when it comes to establishing your online presence, it's a good idea to start out by creating a dedicated website for your business.

To do this, you'll need to register for a domain name and a website host. Sites like squarespace.com and wix.com are great for getting domain names, website hosting, and website templates all in one place. These can be terrific options, especially if you are working on a budget and looking for an easy site builder so you can create your own website – without having to hire a website developer right away.

If you already have a website design, sites like godaddy.com and bluehost.com are highly rated when it comes to domain names and website hosting. Each of these sites will guide you step-by-step on what you need to do on their platforms to set up your website (or transfer an existing site).

While there are many different pages and types of content you can feature on your website, you want to make sure it at least includes these core pages. Be sure to check them off on your own website:

☐	**Homepage.** Your homepage is typically the first point of entry for many customers who visit your website, so you want to make sure you are putting your best foot forward. It should be visually pleasing, easy to navigate, and have clearly visible links to all your other core pages. On your homepage, you want to share a brief overview of your business, showcase your best products and services, and share a couple of your favorite testimonials or reviews. You can even highlight a snippet of your brand story.
☐	**About page.** Your about page is likely to be another one of your most-visited pages. If a customer has never done business with you before, they will visit this page to learn more about who is behind the business as a way to establish credibility and a level of comfort before they make a purchase. The about page is a great opportunity to share more about who you are, your company mission and values, and your brand story, as we went over earlier.
☐	**Products and/or services page(s).** Here's your chance to make your products or services really shine. This is the perfect location to feature photos of your products (or your service in action), detailed descriptions, the benefits of each product or service, how they are different than your competition, and why your ideal customer should buy from you. If you have multiple products or services, you can also categorize them accordingly on this page and link out to their subcategory pages if needed, making all the information easy to find.
☐	**FAQ page.** Having a page dedicated to your frequently asked questions (FAQs) is a great idea. Not only will having this page save you a ton of time (since you won't have to repeat these answers over and over again), but each answer you provide is also an opportunity to convince a potential customer to purchase from you by eliminating any doubts they might have. It's certainly worth the time to create this page. You can start by brainstorming questions yourself, and adding any new ones as your customers actually start asking them.

☐	**Testimonials page.** Great and authentic testimonials can be an excellent credibility and sales tool for your business. The best testimonials will highlight a customer's experience of how your product and/or service positively impacted them. Showcasing real people (with photos, names, social media profiles, etc.) can really help to drive home the impact and authenticity of your testimonials and inspire your ideal customer to make a purchase.
☐	**Blog.** Having a blog is something that is essential to any business (in my opinion). Your blog is a great place to create content on a variety of topics relevant to your business, thus allowing you to showcase your expertise and passion for your field. If executed properly, your blog can be your most effective marketing tool, because it can drive traffic to your site, establish credibility, and in turn convert your blog readers into valuable leads and sales.
☐	**Press and updates page.** If you've been featured by any media, this is a great place to share those accomplishments. For instance, you can include links to articles, videos, podcasts, or social posts that have mentioned your business. This page acts as another way to establish trust and build credibility with your ideal customers.
☐	**Contact and customer service page.** It's important to have an easy-to-find page providing the information customers need to get in contact with you to ask questions or report issues. It also makes it easy for people to reach out to you for media and collaboration opportunities. Be sure to include an email address (or a form that goes to a frequently checked email address), your social media handles if applicable, and a phone number (if you choose).
☐	**Privacy policy, terms and conditions, and disclosures pages.** In today's world, where privacy is constantly being invaded, terms and conditions are often unclear, and disclosures are not being disclosed (no pun intended), you want to be transparent and put your customers' minds at ease. Differentiate yourself from the competition by letting visitors to your site know how any personal information and data they provide will be used, the terms and conditions they'll need to agree to if they choose to browse your site or make a purchase, and any other pertinent information they should be aware of. Ideally, these can be set up as individual pages accessible from the footer section of your website. There are also many legal sites like nolo.com and legalzoom.com that provide templates for these pages that you can customize specifically to your location and business.

Creating a Content Strategy

Establishing a content strategy is an integral part of marketing your business. It specifically refers to how you'll lay out, distribute, and manage the different pieces of content you create for your business. Your content allows your ideal customer to get to know you and your brand, showcases your expertise in your industry, and educates potential customers.

Content comes in a variety of forms, including written content (blog posts and social media captions), visual content (Instagram and Pinterest posts), video content (YouTube, TikTok), and audio content (podcasts). What you decide to create really depends on what's easiest to get started with and what resonates with your target audience (which you'll fine-tune over time based on how people respond). As you consider what form of content to create, you want to take into consideration the following:

- Who is consuming your content (keep your customer avatars in mind)
- The problem are you solving for your ideal customers
- Your unique perspectives and angles for the content you'll create
- The forms of content you will create (blog posts, photos or infographics, podcast episodes, videos, etc.)
- The channels you will use to showcase or share your content

You'll need to spend some time brainstorming different content ideas and doing research for each piece of content you create to make sure it will resonate with your audience, and they'll be able to find it if they search with hashtags, keywords, etc. It's not a bad idea to see what kind of content your competition is creating (or not creating).

A key topic to read up on and learn more about is search engine optimization (SEO), which is essentially the process of improving your site to increase its visibility for relevant searches. One of my favorite websites with a ton of free resources is moz.com (look up their beginner's guide to SEO). Some of my favorite books on SEO and content creation in general (that are totally worth reading) are *Content Inc.* by Joe Pulizzi and *Top of Mind* by John Hall.

Once your content strategy is in place – you've defined your core content ideas, what forms you'll create, and which platforms you'll use to share it – you'll need to create some form of content management process. Enter your content schedule.

Your content schedule. Your content schedule is the second part of your content strategy. It is basically an established plan of when and where you will be publishing the content you create. If you don't have a content schedule in place, you might find that you forget to create content, or don't do it as often as you could. Having a content schedule in place allows you to plan your content ahead of time and stay organized.

As a business owner, this is particularly important if you are juggling a full-time job or other life obligations like being a mom or caregiver. It also makes sure you have the opportunity to plan out and get ahead on content tied to specific holidays and other high-sales seasons that could potentially bring in extra revenue for your business. It shows you the big picture of what's coming up. Plus, if you find that you need to hire support as your business grows, your content schedule is essentially part of a transferable process you can delegate.

Your content schedule can be divided into two parts for organization purposes – your editorial content and your promotional content. Your editorial content is the content you create to educate and inform your audience, show life behind the scenes at your business, tell a story, and so on. Your promotional content is the content specifically tied to sales, offers, any seasonal campaigns you are running, and any content promoting your products and services.

Once you've laid out what kind of content you'll be publishing, the next step is to develop a calendar of specific dates to publish and share each piece of content on each of the platforms you've selected. To easily keep track of your upcoming planned content, you can build a simple Google Sheet or Excel spreadsheet with columns that highlight the specific details or link to the content, the platform where it will be published, the target publication date, its completion status, and a date to republish the content if applicable.

You can also leverage project management tools like Asana or Trello to create your calendar and keep track of the tasks involved. There are also tools like Later Media, HootSuite, SmarterQueue, and Buffer, which allow you to automate your scheduling process by setting them to post content on your chosen date and time (or notifying you to post).

Again, it's a good idea to start with just one platform, and only add more once you've gotten into the swing of things and have established your content creation and scheduling flow.

Now that you know how to create a content strategy and content schedule, it's time to get yours going!

Leverage the suggestions in this section to create your own content strategy. Start by answering these questions:

What is your unique take and angle to add your own spin to create content based on your target customer and the problem you are solving for them?
What forms of content will you create? (Examples include blog posts, social media images, podcast episodes, and videos.)
Which social channels will you use to showcase or share your content?

Once your content strategy is in place, take some time to lay out your content schedule. Write down which content creation tasks you plan to do daily, weekly, and monthly. Build these tasks into your calendar to create a schedule and set reminders.

Business Content Schedule Template

(Add checkmarks to the content creation cadence that works best for you.)

Content type	Daily	Weekly	Monthly

☐	On a calendar, assign specific dates to publish and share each piece of content you create on each of the platforms you've selected. You can use the calendar feature in a project management tool like Asana or Trello or the scheduling feature of the social media platform you are creating the content for.
☐	Set reminders to frequently review and update your calendar. This way you can plan ahead for seasonal initiatives, holidays, and your personal schedule, while still creating informational content to keep your business top-of-mind for your ideal customer.

Setting Your Marketing Goals

A successful strategy starts with you outlining specific and measurable marketing and sales goals you want to achieve and setting a timeline to accomplish them. Having goals in place gives you a "north star" to help track the progress of your strategy and adjust it as needed based on the results you get. Your marketing goals could revolve around promoting new products or services, establishing your brand, targeting new customers, upselling to existing customers, increasing your sales, or maximizing your profits. (After all, the whole point of marketing boils down to getting customers and making money!)

Once you've laid out your marketing goals, the next step is to determine what specific marketing strategies you can test out and implement to help you achieve those goals.

Marketing Strategies to Achieve Your Goals

There are a variety of marketing strategies that, if executed the right way, can help your business grow, get you in front of new customers, and increase your sales and profits. While there is no guarantee that a marketing strategy will work, it's worth testing out a few to determine what methods are most successful and then make tweaks and adjustments to improve their outcomes. Let's get into some of the popular marketing strategies to help you level up your business game.

Social media marketing. I mentioned this earlier as part of creating your content strategy (which also ties into marketing), but it's worth mentioning again because social media marketing is incredibly important in today's world, where people own multiple devices and are constantly online. This means there are so many platforms and opportunities to catch and keep your ideal client's attention and reach audiences that you otherwise would not be able to. Popular social media content platforms at the time of this writing are Facebook, Instagram, YouTube, TikTok, and Pinterest.

Email marketing. Unlike social media marketing, email marketing is all about building an email list of potential customers whom you can communicate with and promote to at any given time. Your email marketing initiatives are not impacted by algorithms, because this is a list you own, so this can be a great way to promote your expertise and your business.

With email marketing, it's important that you don't overwhelm your subscribers with too many emails too quickly. You do, however, want to be consistent with your emails to stay top-of-mind with your audience, but limit yourself to sending them once a week or biweekly so people don't get annoyed and unsubscribe. You should also only email people who have opted into your email list. Adding people to your list who did not opt in can negatively impact your brand image and make it more likely for your emails to be marked as spam. You also don't want to buy email lists for these same reasons. At the end of the day, you want to build an email list that is engaged, wants to hear from you, values your business, and loves your brand.

Paid advertising. This is essentially paying for promotional product or service content placement, either online or in traditional media (radio, television, etc.). Today, it's more common (and cost-effective) for people to leverage social media for their paid advertising strategy. Facebook ads, Instagram ads, TikTok ads, YouTube ads, Pinterest ads, and so on are all relatively easy to set up, and your ad spend can be customized specifically for your budget.

Each of these platforms now has step-by-step tutorials on how to set up ads, and there are plenty of free resources online that can guide you through it and provide extra tips for success. If you choose to do paid marketing, it's worth spending the time to learn how it works and how to set it up yourself (unless you have a massive budget and want to hire someone to manage it for you).

With paid advertising, you'll want to lean on your customer avatar to determine the audiences you want to target, and then run a series of variations (ad tests) to help you determine what ad type is resonating best (and at the lowest cost) with your target audience.

Collaborations. Another great way to market your business (and one that has really helped Clever Girl Finance grow) is collaborations. This could mean partnering with businesses in parallel spaces or partnering with bigger or smaller brands to cross-promote your brands to each other's audiences. The great thing about collaborations is that there are so many ways to do it. You could do joint brand giveaways, content exchange series, guest posts on one another's blogs, a joint online or in-person event – the opportunities are endless.

Events. Online and in-person events are another great marketing strategy. Not only do you get to market your brand and your products or services, but you also have the opportunity to network directly with your ideal customers. This is an incredible way for them to learn more about you and vice versa. Talking to your customers lets you gain valuable insights about who they are and what they want, which in turn can help you fine-tune your customer avatars, improve your products and services, and adjust your marketing strategy.

Giveaways. Running giveaways of your products and services can help to grow your audience by exposing new people to your brand for the first time. However, it's important to clearly outline your goals for the giveaway, because they may attract people who are just looking for free stuff and won't necessarily become loyal brand followers. As a result, some of this audience can quickly dissipate once the giveaway has concluded. Examples of giveaway goals could be creating product or service awareness, leveraging a free product or service to promote a priced product or service, or simply growing your audience. You also want to make sure that any giveaways you choose to run aren't going to cost you too much. You can reduce costs by running a contest-style giveaway, where an unlimited number of people can enter and just a few will win your prizes. This is also a potential way to get more email list subscribers.

Word of mouth. This marketing strategy is by far the most effective because it's all about people telling their friends and family about your products and services. The reason it works so well is that people are more likely to buy from a business if they get a personal recommendation, especially if they are not yet familiar with the business. They know they can trust the word of their relative or friend, and that goes a lot further than even the best advertisement could. I definitely value personal recommendations and make a lot of my purchases that way if it's not a mainstream or popular brand that I already know. People also tend to ask their personal circle whether anyone has heard of a certain brand before they make a first purchase, so word of mouth can be beneficial in this scenario as well.

These are just a few marketing strategies that you can start to test out, fine-tune, and leverage to grow your business. Start with one and go from there! The perfect market strategy is the one that works effectively – not just to attract your ideal customer but to motivate them to make a purchase from you!

Outline some specific marketing goals that you'd like to pursue for your side hustle. Whether it's growing your audience, creating brand awareness, or increasing sales, defining your goals first is foundational to your marketing strategy.

Write out your top 3–5 marketing goals
1
2

3	
4	
5	

☐	Next, select a marketing strategy based on the ideas in this section to begin implementing and build a timeline for how long you want to test this strategy.
☐	Schedule time once a week, biweekly, or at the very least monthly to review the results, and to make tweaks and adjustments to your strategy as necessary.
☐	Add on additional strategies to test out. Rinse and repeat the test cycle and take notes on what marketing methods are proving most successful.

CHAPTER 27

Your Business Finances

I f you don't have a proper plan in place for your business finances, then the money you earn will find ways to slip through your fingers (which is what money does best if you aren't telling it what to do!). If that happens, you'll find that you've spent all this time (long hours and no sleep) working a business, and for what? Plus, let's not forget the regret of wasted time!

The state of your business finances can make or break your business, and it's not just about how much money you are making. You can have the most innovative business idea, a killer brand, and a business plan or marketing strategy that's totally on point, but if your business finances are not in order, your business will eventually crumble and fall apart. Having a solid financial foundation in place for your business should not be optional. It's something that you absolutely have to do if you want to succeed.

It all boils down to money and knowing how to properly manage the finances around your business. I see way too many people running side hustles who sidestep or overlook this all-too-important and very essential piece of the business success puzzle.

Yes, you have your amazing business idea that is going to give you the opportunity to pursue your true passion and let you do what you really love. This is the hustle that's going to get you out of the nine-to-five and into your dream life, and you've seen it all play out in your

---

Note: To download printable pdf and Excel versions of the business finance worksheets in this section, visit clevergirlfinance.com/my-wealth-plan.

head. You have been following the action steps in this workbook and you are ready to build your empire. But before you go off spending tons of money on branding, production, and marketing, let's take some time to break down what it's really going to cost you.

Estimating Your Startup Expenses

To establish a solid plan, we need to start at the very beginning by estimating your startup expenses, aka startup costs.

If your business is already up and running, you can skip ahead to the section right after this one that covers operating expenses. However, it could still be valuable for you to read this section, because knowing how much you spent setting up your business gives you the opportunity to reflect on those costs, review the foundations of your business finances, and gauge your progress over time.

Your startup expenses are the costs you incur to get your business up and running. They are different from your operating expenses, which are recurring expenses that you typically pay every month, quarter, or year.

For instance, a startup expense could be website design, because this is typically a one-time expense you'll have to pay – you won't be redesigning your website every single month. On the other hand, an operating expense could be website hosting – a fee you'll pay on a monthly basis to keep your website actively visible online.

Being intentional about your startup costs lets you create an initial spending plan to get your business up and running. It also acts as the beginning of your business budget. As your business becomes profitable, you'll be able to compare your baseline startup costs against your current revenue to judge how much financial progress you've made to keep you on track.

Lay Out Your Startup Costs

As you think about your startup costs, here are my suggestions around what startup expenses a business owner should be considering. You can fill in the gaps as it relates to your own specific business using the next worksheet:

- Domain name registration (e.g. www.xyz.com)
- Custom email accounts (e.g. info@xyz.com)
- Business registration fees (state and federal)
- Trademark fees (state and federal)

- Branding (logo and fonts)
- Website design
- Initial website hosting fees
- Initial advertising/marketing expenses
- Initial certifications or courses
- Equipment (computer, printer/scanner)
- Office supplies
- Product samples
- Initial product inventory

Once you have your necessary startup expenses all laid out, be sure to price out each item on your list. This way, you'll have a good idea of how much money you'll need to fund your business initially to get it off the ground, and you'll also have a baseline to measure against.

Startup expense type	Category	Description	Estimated amount	Actual amount

Startup expense type	Category	Description	Estimated amount	Actual amount
		TOTAL	$	$

Creating a Functional Business Budget

In order to build out a functional business budget, you'll need to understand your baseline operating expenses, lay out a budget, and have a good sense of forecasting your business income and expenses month to month. That's what we'll go over next.

Understanding Your Operating Expenses

The next set of expenses you'll have are your operating costs. These are the expenses that are incurred on an ongoing basis to keep your business running. They are important to be aware of, because these are the expenses that will most likely be coming your way every single month, and you need to plan for them so you can pay for them.

Your operating expenses can be broken down into two categories: fixed operating expenses and variable operating expenses. Let's go over each type so you can plan for them accordingly.

- **Your fixed operating expenses.** These are expenses that typically do not change from month to month, regardless of your business sales or production changes. Some examples of fixed operating expenses include business insurance, internet services, tools subscriptions, website hosting fees, virtual assistant fees, and rent.
- **Your variable operating expenses.** These expenses vary from month to month because they are directly tied to your business activity – for instance, having higher or lower product manufacturing needs. Variable costs can include the raw materials for your products, inventory management, production costs, third-party payment processing tools, shipping fees, advertising fees, and event expenses.

If you have quarterly or annual operating expenses, you can divide them by 3 (for quarterly, since there are three months in each quarter) or 12 months (for annual expenses) to determine your true monthly expenses. As a very simplistic example, you might have one $100/month cost, one $600/quarter cost (divides to $200/month), and one $3600/year cost (divides to $300/month). In this example, your true monthly expenses are $600.

You also want to keep in mind that as your business grows or as you start offering new products and services, your variable operating expenses will most likely grow with these additions, while your fixed expenses will remain the same. Once you've mapped out what your operating expenses truly are, you'll be able to build them into your monthly business budget and forecast them as accurately as possible.

Categorizing Your Operating Expenses

Once you've determined exactly what your operating expenses are, it's a good idea to group them into categories. You are likely to have several different types of expenses as you grow your side hustle, and by categorizing them appropriately, you'll be able to see very quickly which categories are driving your highest and also your lowest costs. It also makes it easier to build out your business budget when you have specific categories designated. For example, things like Facebook ads would fall under the expense category of advertising or marketing. If you hire someone to do paid graphic design work for you, that expense could fall under branding. For each of your categories, you can add a detailed description of what each expense was for.

As you categorize your expenses, you can use your own categories, but make sure you or your accountant can easily map them to the IRS business categories for tax purposes.

According to quickbooks.com and based on IRS guidance, some common business expense categories include:

- Advertising and marketing
- Bank charges and fees
- Car and truck
- Commissions and fees, e.g. sales or referral commissions
- Contractors
- Dues and subscriptions
- Home office expenses
- Insurance
- Interest paid
- Licenses and fees
- Legal fees and professional services
- Meals and entertainment
- Office expenses
- Payroll expenses
- Rent and lease
- Repairs and maintenance
- Shipping and delivery
- Supplies
- Taxes and licenses
- Travel expenses
- Utilities
- Other business expenses that don't fit into any of the mentioned expense categories

Your operating expenses and your expense categories are things you'll need to identify early on in order to properly plan out your business finances. Mapping them out now helps you know what to expect and plan for later.

If you are a new business owner, you can do a review of your business plan and take some time to talk to some tenured business owners in your field to find out the types of expenses they have on a monthly basis. Alternatively, you can do some Google research to get a few ideas.

If you are a tenured business owner, I'd suggest going over a few months of business bank statements or reviewing whatever business accounting files you have. These will give you an idea of your historic operating expenses so you can decide what to keep or cut from your budget going forward.

Your operating expenses should also be reviewed on a monthly basis as part of your business budget review process (which we'll get into in the next section). These are expenses that can easily get out of control, especially as your business grows. If you don't keep an eye on them, expenses can quickly creep up and start eating into your business income and profits.

You can use a simple spreadsheet or simplified accounting software like FreshBooks, WaveApps, Xero, or QuickBooks Online, among others, to track your expenses and keep them organized in categories when you're starting out. As your business grows, it's a good idea to consult with a bookkeeper or accountant to make sure you're on the right track.

Your Business Budget

The same way you have a budget for your personal finances, you need to have a budget for your business finances. When you create a budget, you are essentially telling your money what to do on a daily, weekly, and monthly basis to grow your business and allow you to achieve your financial goals.

Your business budget is basically your money plan for your business, so having one is essential to managing your business finances successfully. Your budget will guide the expenditures you make in your business and help you stay on top of your business spending. I can't stress how important this is!

When you want to buy groceries, you create a list and reference the amount you have allocated to spend in your budget before you head out to the grocery store, right? (If your answer is "umm," "I don't know," or "Don't talk to me," now is a great time for you to pick up my first book, *Clever Girl Finance: Ditch Debt, Save Money and Build Real Wealth*!)

You are probably very familiar with the fact that if you don't create a grocery list and you don't reference your budget, you can easily get distracted by all kinds of "amazing" food items at the store, load up your cart with more than you need, and return home as the not-so-proud owner of the entire aisle 16. Listen, you are not alone; I can totally relate because I've been there and done that. . .and yes, I've got the T-shirt (again) to prove it!

When you reference your budget, you are more likely to stick to your grocery list and you may even have money left over to put toward other categories in your budget, like saving or investing!

Well, the same thing applies to your business. If you wanted to create a new product, you'd make a list of all the things you need to create it and reference your budget to determine how much you can (or cannot) allocate to this project to get started. On the other hand, if you don't have a plan and just "spend as you go," you are likely to run out of money, eat into profits, or put your business into an unnecessary financial bind. Over time, this lack of budgeting can put you out of business and deep into debt. Thus, having a business budget is super-important because you can properly allocate your financial resources, stay focused on achieving profitability as quickly as possible, build up a buffer of savings, and invest in growing your business over time.

Keep in mind that having a business budget is not always the same as using an accounting tool or software. While some accounting tools offer business budgeting features, most just track your actual spending and expenses. Your budget, on the other hand, allows you to plan ahead so you can see the full picture before you spend.

However, before we talk about how to create a business budget, we first have to discuss the importance of ensuring that your business finances are kept separate from your personal finances.

Keeping Your Business and Personal Finances Separate

Although you can use your personal money to fund your business initially, you need to ensure that you have separate bank accounts for your personal life and for your business and that you are keeping your financial transactions completely separate.

For one thing, keeping your finances separate will help you clearly understand how your business is really performing. In addition (and very importantly), keeping your finances separate will help you avoid any issues with the IRS, which has strict rules around business financials and how they are tracked for tax purposes. Separate financials will also prevent you from violating any operating terms based on the type of legal entity you have (e.g. an LLC or a corporation).

Co-mingling your finances can be confusing, cause you to pay more taxes than necessary, and even get you in trouble with the IRS (high penalties and back-calculated interest) – and you definitely don't want any problems with Uncle Sam!

If you are using personal funds to start your business, here are four key tips:

1. **Adjust your personal budget to account for the funds you'll be putting into your business.** This way, you won't impact your other expenses and personal finance goals and you can plan

accordingly. If you are using a credit card, make sure the credit card is designated only for business expenses.

Caution: When leveraging debt to start a business, it's essential that you have created a strategy of how you'll be paying this debt back.

2. **You can designate the personal funds you deposit into your business as an equity investment in your business or as a loan from you to your business that your business has to repay back to you in the future.** Be sure to keep track of the dates and the specific amounts.

3. **Deposit the designated personal funds into your business account.** From there, make all your business transactions using your business account, not your personal account.

4. **When your business starts to make money, you have a couple of options.** You can either reinvest the earnings back into your business so your business can become self-sustaining or create a plan to pay yourself back the loan you made to your business.

To open your business accounts, you'll need your Employer Identification Number (EIN), the official paperwork for your registered business, and one or more forms of personal identification (depending on what the specific bank requires). If you are unsure, you should consult with an accountant to help you set up these structures.

With that being said, let's get back to budgeting. There are two key steps to creating a solid business budget: forecasting your income and forecasting your expenses. Let's go over each one.

Forecasting Your Business Income

As part of your budgeting process, you want to be able to forecast your potential business income, as well as track your actual income so you know how much your business can potentially earn versus how much it is actually earning. While you may not be able to perfectly predict your business income, here are a few steps you can take:

- **Compare your business to other existing businesses.** If you can, talk to owners of tenured businesses to find out what their sales were like when they were at your stage as well as what they did to drive those sales.
- **Determine what types of activities could drive sales for you.** For instance, is there a certain type of advertising you can do? Can you restructure your services or repackage your products in a certain way?
- **Base your forecast on volume.** How many products will you need to sell to make X amount of money?

Again, there's no exact science to forecasting your business income and it's not meant to be 100% accurate. The goal of forecasting your income is to get you thinking, planning, and researching how much money you could make. Don't be afraid to create different scenarios. The most important thing to keep in mind with forecasting is that you want to set reasonable expectations for what your business can realistically earn over a period of time, given what you know and the specific action steps you can take to drive those earnings.

Forecasting Your Business Expenses

Similar to forecasting your income, you can also forecast your expenses. This step is a lot more straightforward than forecasting income, since you can't see the future and know how many sales you'll make, but you can easily research what things cost. When you create the expenses section of your business budget, you'll need to pull in the list of startup and/or operating expenses you created earlier. Once you've done this, the next thing you want to do is assign amounts to them (if you haven't already) and think through any potential reasons why your expenses could increase for a given month.

Your fixed expenses will not change much, unless you expect to add any brand-new fixed expenses. However, your variable expenses can be forecasted based on what expenses you think will increase based on your business growth or due to seasonality. For instance, if you expect a potential to sell 10% more products in a month (e.g. in a month with a holiday sale weekend) and you accept PayPal payments, then you can expect to have 10% more in additional PayPal commission expenses as well. On the other hand, if you expect a slow month, your variable expenses might be lower, but you should plan to have enough savings to cover your fixed expenses (since these won't typically decrease).

Again, these exercises are just designed to get you thinking and researching. For instance, if you're starting a wedding photography business, you can look up peak wedding months versus slower seasons to help forecast your income and expenses.

Tracking Profits and Loss

For a business owner, while breaking even is great, you ultimately want to earn profits – and a lot of them. In the early stages of your business, it's likely that your monthly business expenses may exceed your monthly business income for a while. This is normal, but it makes tracking your income against your expenses very important, because it allows you to see how close to (or far away from) earning a profit you are each month.

Regardless of what stage you've reached in your business, you want to track both your income and your expenses in your business budget so you can ensure you are keeping your expenses within your budget and aren't consistently operating in the red each month. Every dollar you spend in your business eats into your profits (or adds debt if you aren't yet profitable). And when you aren't tracking your spending, it's easy for money to disappear fast.

As business owners, we are sometimes guilty of disguising our over-spending as "needs" for the business. From paid tools that you think will make your life easier, to fancy office accessories and furniture so your photos look cute for the 'gram or TikTok, to upgrading features on your products and services that your customers may barely even notice, money can easily slip away and eliminate profits if you are not careful.

Keeping track of your profits versus your expenses can help you gain valuable insights about which specific areas in your business are driving the biggest profits or losses. These insights in turn can help you determine if you are overspending in certain areas that have minimal returns and if there is an opportunity to cut back in those areas. They can also help you determine which specific products or services are earning you more money than others. You can use this knowledge to focus on further promoting your best sellers as well as finding ways to improve, revise, or discontinue the products or services that aren't performing that well.

You can leverage your business budget to analyze your profits and loss by setting your budget up in a way where it also tracks the actual sales of your individual products and services.

To analyze your profits and losses, you would focus specifically on the "actual amounts" for both your income (broken out by specific product and service) and your expenses. Your actual income minus your actual expenses will show you your overall profit or loss for a given month. Then you can narrow in on each product and service category to determine which ones drove the profits or losses. A good accounting software can also help you create a profit-and-loss report based on your business transactions.

Putting Your Business Budget Together

Now it's time to create your business budget. This is exciting – you are creating a plan that can make all the difference when it comes to the financial success of your business! (I know *budget* and *exciting* aren't often used in the same sentence but stick with me!)

Creating your business budget doesn't have to be complicated, especially if you are just getting started. You can put it together in a simple spreadsheet with basic formulas. When laying out your budget, you want to include your expected or forecasted monthly business income as well as your monthly business expenses (including your startup costs if you are a new business owner and your recurring monthly operating expenses).

To make it easier, you can break things up into some categories, as discussed earlier, to keep things organized.

Leverage the tips in this section to create your business budget and get ready to track your business income and expenses.

- You can build out your budget for several months at a time so you can plan, project, and forecast your business financials in advance. Be sure to review and adjust your budget as needed at least once a month, paying special attention to your expenses.
- Be aware of all your operating costs (i.e. how much you need to keep your business up and running each month).
- As you run your business, set a reminder at the end of each month to review your budget and do a profit-and-loss assessment to gain additional insights for your business growth.

Simple Monthly Side Hustle/Business Budget Worksheet

Month: _____

Income category	Income description	Expected/fore-casted amount	Actual amount	Difference (±)
	Total	$	$	$

Expense category	Expense description	Budgeted amount	Actual amount	Difference (±)
	Total	$	$	$

Monthly Profit/Loss (Actual income – Actual expenses)	$

This template, with preset formulas, is available to download at clevergirlfinance.com/my-wealth-plan.

Remember, your business budget is a tool and reference that you are creating for the success of your business, so you want to make sure it makes sense to you.

Building Taxes into Your Budget

One important thing to keep in mind is that when your business starts to earn profits, you are likely to owe taxes to the government, so it's a good idea to build your potential tax obligation into your budget as an expense. A good rule of thumb, if you are unsure of your exact business tax obligation, is to set aside 25–30% of your business profits toward taxes in a designated business savings account. This way, you can cover your tax obligation without putting a strain on your business finances. If you have extra funds left over after tax season, you can reinvest the money back into your business or keep saving it for a rainy day.

It's also recommended that you make quarterly tax payments based on your estimated tax obligation. Per the IRS.gov website, "Taxes must be paid as you earn or receive income during the year, either through withholding or estimated tax payments." It also states, "Individuals, including sole proprietors, partners, and S corporation shareholders, generally have to make estimated tax payments if they expect to owe tax of $1,000 or more when their return is filed."

An accountant can help you determine your specific tax rate and guide you as to how much you should be putting aside toward your tax obligation.

▶ Plan Ahead

You should plan to create your business budget in advance of each month. You can also create it for several months at a time and review things again ahead of each month.

Once your budget is created, you want to make use of it by tracking your actual business spending against the budget you set, taking note of any variances or reasons why your budget came in over or under. This should be something you do often. It's a good idea to build a budget check-in into your weekly schedule.

Breaking Even: Profit and Loss

Your business budget is the foundation of your finances, but there are other elements that are extremely important to track as well.

Specifically, you need to understand how to determine your break-even point and calculate your business profit and loss. Let's start with how you can perform a break-even analysis for your products and services in a simple way.

Performing a Break-Even Analysis

Performing a break-even analysis helps you determine how much your business needs to sell to cover its total expenses (both fixed and variable) before it can become profitable. However, in order to successfully perform a break-even analysis, you need to know what your expected income is, as well as what your total expenses are. Once you know how much you need to sell in one month to break even (aka making enough to cover all your expenses, but not yet making a profit), you can set that as a business sales goal and start working toward it.

A simple formula you can use to perform a break-even analysis is as follows:

Your total fixed expenses
  DIVIDED BY (÷)
  The price of your products or services

  MINUS (−)
  The variable costs to produce each product or service

  EQUALS (=)
  The number of products or services you need to sell to break even

Let's go over this formula again with a realistic example. Let's say for the next 12 months, the total fixed expenses for your business come out to $5000 and you have one product type that you will be selling for $20 per product. You've also determined that the variable cost to produce each product is $5, based on various factors, including the price of supplies for the specific time period. Based on these numbers and the formula we are using, the number of products you would need to sell in order to break even would be:

$$\$5,000 \div (\$20.00 - \$5.00) = \text{about } 333 \text{ products}$$

You can take the formula above and test it out for yourself, using your total fixed expenses, the price of your products or services, and the variable costs associated with producing your products and services.

Here's a simple worksheet where you can apply this break-even formula. Use the number you get to establish your initial sales goals.

Break-Even Analysis Worksheet

Product name	Total fixed expenses	Price of product or service	Variable cost to produce product or service	# of products or services to sell to break even
Example: Product 1	$1000	$50	$10	25

This template, with preset formulas, is available at clevergirlfinance.com/my-wealth-plan.

Keep in mind that the variable costs associated with your products or services can change due to factors outside of your control – for instance, a change in the cost of supplies. You also want to keep in mind that the amount you use for your total fixed expenses should be based on the timeframe in which you want to break even. For example, if you use your total fixed expenses for one month in this calculation, then the result you get will be the number of products you need to sell to break even in one month.

Pricing Your Products and Services

One of the biggest challenges business owners face is charging appropriately for their products and services. I personally struggled with this in the early stages of my various side hustles. When it came to pricing my products and services, I worried whether I was charging too much, so I ended up giving excessive discounts or not charging at all (especially with friends and family). As I scaled my businesses, I felt guilty about increasing my prices. Sometimes I was even put in awkward positions of having to say no to people who attempted to haggle my pricing even after I had clearly stated what my prices were. *Ugh*. . .the worst.

The problem with charging too low is that people may not associate the right value with your products and services. Essentially, cheap pricing may cause them to think your products are also cheap or not of good quality. If you have an amazing product or service, this perception could cause you to lose out on potential sales.

On the flipside, setting your pricing too high could also cause you to lose out on potential sales because your ideal customer is just not willing to pay that much. This can happen for a combination of reasons, like the perceived value of your products and services (just like with charging too low), whom you are targeting, and what your competition is charging.

I personally had to learn how to determine the right pricing strategies for my business and how to say no when people were trying to take advantage of a personal relationship they had with me to get a discount or a freebie. While it was difficult to figure things out initially, this process only served me for the better when it came to growing my business and my profits.

If you are nodding your head because you can relate to all of this in one way or another, let's talk through how to price your products and services with strategies that actually work.

When it comes to pricing, there are a number of different strategies you can test and choose from. This way, you are not just assigning prices blindly with the hopes that maybe, just maybe, someone will buy from you.

By leveraging a proven pricing strategy, you can assign the best prices to your products and services, get paid what you are worth, and maximize your profits while still remaining attractive to your ideal customers and staying competitive in your space. So let's get into some common, effective pricing strategies!

- **Cost pricing strategy.** This strategy is ideal for product-based businesses. You'll start by calculating what it costs you to create each product. Once you've determined the cost per product, you can then add a markup to the price to include the total amount of profit you'd like to earn on each product. For example, let's say you sell scented candles, each candle costs you $12 to create, and you'd like to earn a minimum profit of $5 per candle. Your sales price would be $17 per candle.
- **Competitive pricing strategy.** With this strategy, your pricing is based on how your competitors are pricing similar products or services. By pricing your products and services slightly lower than your competitors, you can gain a competitive edge. This strategy can be

beneficial if your products or services are in a highly saturated business industry.

- **Discount pricing strategy.** This strategy is all about selling a product or service at a specific price normally but lowering the pricing during specific periods of time. For instance, you can offer discounts during a particular time of year (e.g. summer), during popular sales seasons (e.g. Black Friday), or when a product or service is being discontinued.

- **Premium pricing strategy.** This pricing strategy focuses on high-value brands with high perceived brand value. If you have established a solid and compelling brand identity, your perceived brand value can make up the difference for higher pricing.

- **What your customer is willing to pay.** With this pricing strategy, you intentionally sell your products and services based on what your ideal customer is willing to pay, which you can determine by researching and collecting data. One simple way to collect this data is to run surveys where your ideal customers can answer questions or select preset ranges of how much they might pay for specific a product or service.

- **Bundle pricing strategy.** Bundling products and services can be an effective pricing strategy because with a bundle you can compel a customer to buy more at a lower per-product cost than if they were to buy the products individually.

- **Freemium pricing strategy.** This pricing strategy is based on the idea that if you offer a free but valuable product or service add-on, you can compel your customer to pay for or upgrade to a full-priced product or service. For instance, "buy one get one free," "buy and get a free gift," and "try for free and upgrade for more" are all ways to leverage this freemium approach.

- **Psychology-based pricing.** This pricing approach is something that works on all of us subconsciously without our even realizing it. It could be the perceived lower value of a product or service because it's priced with a .99 or a .95 at the end. Or it could be a placement approach, where a lower-cost product or service is featured next to a higher-cost product or service, with the intent to get the customer to purchase the lower-cost offering. Psychological approaches to pricing also include the freemium and bundled pricing strategies as we discussed earlier.

Regardless of whichever pricing strategy you choose, I highly recommend that you always factor in what it costs to create the product or service. I also highly recommend testing out different pricing strategies and variations of the same pricing strategy to determine what works best for you.

Now it's your turn to lay out your pricing strategy:
- Start out by selecting one or two pricing strategies that are relevant to your business and make a plan to begin testing them.
- Gather and assess your results after each test and implement the approach that works best for you.

Pricing strategies to test	Test by date	Notes/Assessment

CHAPTER **28**

Business
Metrics to Track

Your business metrics are basically performance indicators that showcase how well your business is doing. This is extremely important because it can help you get a sense of what's working well (and what's not), what's driving sales, and what needs to be adjusted. All of these insights will help you make better business decisions and track your progress, and they can even help you identify problems before they get out of hand.

You can leverage metrics to track pretty much any part of your business that you want to focus on, but there are some metrics that you may need to look at more closely than others. I would suggest tracking and assessing your metrics on a monthly basis.

Financial Metrics

Some key financial metrics you'll want to pay attention to each month include:

- **Fixed costs.** These are the costs you need to pay for regardless of how your business is doing and essentially represent your overhead. Tracking these helps you stay aware of any cost increases that happen and gives you a baseline for how much revenue you need to make at a minimum to cover these costs.
- **Variable costs.** Your variable costs are typically tied to the creation and production volume of your product and services. Tracking this

metric helps you get a sense of if and how your revenue is changing when your variable costs change.

- **Total sales or revenue.** This metric is one that every business owner should absolutely be tracking so you are aware of how much money your business is making as a whole from your different products and services.
- **Average sales or revenue.** Knowing your average revenue is another metric that is good to track, because you'll be able to compare your average revenue to your monthly costs to see if your revenue is covering your costs on average each month. Sometimes those high months can be deceiving if you also experience low months, so it's a good idea to know and track your averages.
- **Sales goals.** Knowing what your sales goals are for each month, quarter, or year will help you stay on top of tracking your progress when it comes to all the activities required to make the needed sales.
- **Profit margin.** This metric helps you gain a clear picture of what your true profits are when you subtract your expenses from your revenue. The goal is to widen the gap as much as possible between the two, so your revenue exceeds your expenses by a large margin. Tracking this metric will keep you mindful of your expenses and can help you think creatively when it comes to your sales strategies.

Marketing Metrics

Some key marketing metrics that are a good idea to pay attention to include:

- **Customer acquisition rate.** This metric measures the rate at which you are acquiring potential customers from specific activities on your various acquisition channels. For instance, how many people signed up to your email list from reading an article on your website, or from visiting your website via your Instagram profile, or from clicking one of your product images on Pinterest? Knowing your acquisition metrics can help you decide on which channel to focus your time and efforts.
- **Conversion rates.** This metric is defined as the number of conversions (sales, signups, or other desired actions) divided by the total number of visitors. For instance, you can track the number of sales you make based on the number of visitors to your product or services pages via your different customer acquisition channels. Or you could track the number of your Instagram followers who visited your Instagram shop and made a purchase. You can even use

conversion rates to track how effective your Facebook ads are based on the number of sales they return. Knowing your conversion rates can help you fine-tune your marketing strategy.

- **New versus returning customers.** Another good metric to track is your new versus returning customers. Who is visiting your product or service pages and making purchases? Are you getting a lot of repeat customers? Knowing this metric can help you determine if there is an opportunity to retarget either of these customer categories with ads to incentivize them to make additional purchases.

- **Social media engagement.** While this metric does not necessarily translate to sales, it's worth tracking to get a sense of what your customers are talking about and the questions they're asking. This engagement can also give you a sense of brand loyalty. Social media engagement metrics include things like comments, likes, and shares. The insights you gain can be used to improve your marketing strategy and even your products and services. Take note of anything customers are saying about things they wish your product or service had.

Tools to Track Your Business Metrics

Now that we've gone over a baseline list of potential metrics you can track, you're probably wondering exactly how to track each of them. One great way to keep it all in one place is to create a simple spreadsheet that has a list of the metrics you want to track each month.

You can pull metrics from your business budget and from the various analytics and insights features available today on each of the social media platforms. For example, you can leverage the "insights" section of your account on Instagram and the "analytics" section on Pinterest to pull specific metrics you want to track each month.

Another incredibly powerful and free tool that you can use to track how customers are using your website is Google Analytics. This powerful tool can help you analyze your website traffic, which is incredibly important because your website is your home base. You can track the actions visitors take on your website (pages visited, landing pages, exit pages, time spent), gain insights about the demographics of your visitors (age, location, interests, etc.), and even set sales and revenue goals tied to specific products or services on your Google Analytics account. I highly recommend using Google Analytics – it's totally worth the time it takes to set it up for your business website. Google offers a great tutorial for beginners on using Google Analytics, which you can find at https://analytics.google.com/analytics/academy.

Now that you know the importance of tracking your business metrics, get started with yours.

- **Create a list of metrics most relevant to your business goals to begin tracking.**
- Keep in mind that you don't need to track every single metric available, just the ones that are most relevant or impactful to your business right now. You can always add on others later.

1.

2.

3.

4.

5.

6.

7.

8.

9.

10.

11.

12.

☐	**Organize the metrics you want to track in a spreadsheet by month over the next 12 months.** To make it easier, you can set this up as a separate tab, or "sheet," next to your business budget spreadsheet if you are using Microsoft Excel or Google Sheets. You can download the Clever Girl Finance template at clevergirlfinance.com/my-wealth-plan.
☐	**Set up your Google Analytics accounts for your website.** If you are unsure how to do this, check out the free tutorials Google offers at https://analytics.google.com/analytics/academy.
☐	**Schedule recurring time each month to review the metrics you are tracking.** Pay close attention to any trends you see and make a note of any key actions you took throughout each month that affected your metrics. Use this information to brainstorm ideas to grow your future revenue.

CHAPTER **29**

Your Dream Team

When you start a side hustle, you may get to a point where you need that extra support to grow your business. Having an in-person or virtual assistant (VA) can help you with managing tasks and keep things running smoothly. I've always had (and still have) an assistant or VA on my team and their support is invaluable. This extra pair of hands is great for handling administrative duties, customer service, and other day-to-day operations.

However, as your side hustle grows, you might reach a point where you need more specialized skills to continue scaling your business. Whether it's marketing expertise, technical support, or creative input, bringing in professionals with specific talents can help you tackle new challenges and take on more opportunities for growth. And so being able to balance your general support needs with your specialized skill needs is essential for taking your side hustle to the next level.

That said, as you start to think about where you might need help (now or in the future) and how to find the right resources, here is a checklist to help you hire well:

Hiring Checklist

☐	**Identify where you need support.** Based on the different aspects of your business you laid out in the previous section and the specific steps required to complete each category and task, identify where you need help the most and prioritize that need. Do you need a designer, a social media manager, an assistant, a writer, a developer? This exercise will help you get clear on where you have the most pressing need.
☐	**Create your job requirements.** Create a specific job requirement of the skill set each ideal candidate would need to have in order to support you successfully in the different areas you need support.
☐	**Put the word out. Once you are ready to hire,** you can put the word out through your personal network, your business audience/community, by asking for referrals from people you know, or by making a job post on an online freelance platform like fiverr.com, upwork.com, and the like.
☐	**Have hiring contracts in place.** It's also really important to have a contractual agreement in place for anyone you hire so the terms of their employment are clear. This contract should clearly highlight any trial periods (I'd highly recommend at least a 30-day trial period), payment terms, working hours, status (e.g. contractor, part-time, full-time), and the job description. Websites like LegalZoom.com, Rocket Lawyer.com, and Nolo.com offer customizable employment contract templates that you can purchase and download. You can also speak with a business attorney.

Additionally, consider the following:

- **Take your time to hire.** Ever heard the saying *hire slow but fire fast*? Well, it rings true. When you take your time to hire by going through an interview process with potential candidates, taking time to determine if they are a good fit for your brand, checking their references, and speaking with them at least a couple of times, you are less likely to have hiring regrets. It's definitely true that sometimes even if you've done your due diligence, things don't work out, but by taking your time to make your decision, you can minimize your chances of a bad hire.
- **Hire on a contract basis until you can hire part-time or full-time.** Even if you can only hire on an as-needed basis, it can make a huge difference in getting tasks done, especially if you are working on a tight timeline.

As your side hustle grows, having the right team will be essential to its success, so take the time to make smart and strategic hiring decisions.

Finding the Right Mentors

Having mentors with expansive business experience can be extremely helpful, especially when you are trying to figure things out, navigating a difficult period in business, or experiencing amazing growth and need some support or guidance. They can also be the ones to encourage and give you the push you need to take the next big step in your business that might be outside of your comfort zone.

To find these mentors, it's all about relationship building: meeting people and spending time getting to know them. Once you've done this, you want to communicate openly about how you'd like them to support you, while being respectful of their time.

One way to start is within your personal network. Once you get intentional about seeking out mentors, you may be surprised about who you are already connected to within your network.

For instance, some of your friends, acquaintances, or former colleagues may have business ideas or might have even started businesses they have not shared broadly. One of my amazing mentors is actually a former boss of mine who just happens to be a serial entrepreneur with an in-depth knowledge of business strategy and development. But funnily enough, I had no idea about his experience. It wasn't until a couple of years after I left that particular job and was talking to a former coworker about starting a business that they suggested I get reconnected with this particular mentor, and I'm so grateful they made that suggestion.

Another way to seek out mentors is through introductions from people you are connected to. I can't tell you how many great connections I've made from other people introducing me to people within their network, many of whom I am still constantly in touch with.

You can also make time to participate in entrepreneur-focused events (online and in-person), participate in entrepreneur communities and groups, and even engage with other entrepreneurs on social media. Thanks to the Internet and the evolution of social interactions online, it's become so much easier to meet other people. However, it's going to require that you are intentional, and you might need to step out of your comfort zone, especially if you are somewhat introverted like me.

Keep in mind that when it comes to mentors, you can have several for different reasons. I've had people mentor me once, on a sporadic basis and on an ongoing consistent basis over a period of months, and even years. And I've had mentors who have helped me with marketing, business strategy, leadership, speaking, and more.

Finally, you might decide to hire a coach to guide you through certain aspects of building your business. If you choose to go this route, be sure to do your research to make sure they can truly help you, have the experience, and very importantly, that they are a good fit for your personality and style.

How would you need a mentor to support you? If you are looking for a mentor, create a list of specifically how you'd like a mentor to support you.

1.

2.

3.

4.

5.

6.

7.

8.

Next, start with your personal network and ask for introductions from people you are connected to already. You should also seek out and join entrepreneur communities (they could be within your niche and industry) and build potential mentor relationships that way. Leverage the list you've created to guide your discussions as you build your mentor relationships.

PART IV

Choosing to Prosper

CHAPTER 30

Making the Intentional Choice to Prosper

Welcome to the final section of your wealth plan! So far, we've focused on the financial aspect of wealth, which is of course extremely important, but in this next section I'd like you to shift your focus to the type of wealth that goes well beyond money. I'm talking about tapping into your wealth of talent, your wealth of strength, your wealth of perseverance, and your wealth of ambition, all of which tie into and will lead you to prosperity and abundance in all areas of your life.

This section of the workbook is designed to guide you on a transformative journey of self-discovery and growth. Through prompt-driven journaling, you'll be empowered to tap into your thoughts, feelings, and desires, and gain clarity on what drives you. By intentionally focusing on what propels you forward, you'll unlock your potential and cultivate a mindset that embraces prosperity in all aspects of your life. As you commit to this process, you'll build confidence, and develop a deeper understanding of yourself. In turn, you'll emerge with a renewed sense of purpose, confidence, and direction, ready to live a life that truly reflects your highest aspirations.

If you've ever felt undervalued, underestimated, overlooked, or been made to feel less than worthy, the prompts in this section will help you tap into your greater purpose with just the right nudges to gain clarity as you make the intentional choice to prosper. Let's go!

CHAPTER **31**

Who You Are

Reflecting on who and what has shaped you has the power to help you craft your future.

We went over this a little in the first part of this workbook but more specifically as it relates to money. This time I'd like you to take a holistic look back at your background and history, and leverage your assessment to determine how you'd like to craft your future.

Here are a few questions and prompts to help you reflect.

Take a moment to journal about your childhood. What experiences (good or bad) do you remember the most?

Who in your family inspired you the most growing up?

What opportunities do you wish had been available for your family?

What are you choosing to do better or differently to change or improve the narrative for your own future?

Create a one-sentence affirmation that says you deserve whatever it is you desire – financial security, a fulfilling career, healthy relationships, and so on – regardless of your past. Repeat it to yourself every day until you believe it.

Your story is important, and so is reflecting on it in order to determine the type of life you want to live. Be intentional about applying what you know, what you've learned, and what you want to do differently on your journey to crafting the future you truly desire for yourself.

CHAPTER **32**
Coming of Age

Every life experience, while not always positive, is a reminder to be confident in who you are and grow thick skin.

Sometimes certain experiences happen that might make you question who you are or challenge your values. In the moment, you might feel all kinds of emotions, but upon reflection, there are always lessons to learn that can help shape the future you.

Let's go back to some of your earlier days when you were in college or high school and unpack some of those experiences. Here are some questions to help you reflect.

What was a challenging experience you faced in college or high school that made you question your identity or values?

How did you feel during and immediately after the experience? What emotions arose?

What did you learn about yourself and your capabilities from that experience?

How did it shape your perspective on life, relationships, or your goals?

What strengths or resilience did you discover within yourself during that time?

How has that experience influenced your decisions or actions since then?

What wisdom or advice would you give to your younger self navigating that experience?

How has your perspective on the experience changed over time, and what new insights have emerged?

What are some key takeaways or lessons that you can apply to your life now and in the future?

We all have those memories, both pleasant or otherwise, from our high school and college days (and even throughout our lives). As you reflect on yours, focus on how those memories have shaped you and lay out the life lessons you learned from your experiences that you can apply to your personal growth today.

CHAPTER **33**

Your Career Journey

Don't be afraid to be bold on your career path. It might take practice as you step into your own, but remember your self-worth.

The early years of your career can be some of the most defining years of your life, and even if you are beyond those early years, looking back on them can be extremely insightful. It's important to take advantage of and reflect on every opportunity that comes your way that could help you succeed or drive change. Here are some questions to help you reflect on your career so far.

Is there a catalyst on your career path that you have yet to recognize? For me, it was finding out that most of my peers had negotiated higher salaries. What is it for you?

Do you feel like you need to be more intentional about your career goals? In what way?

Are there opportunities in your workplace that are staring right at you that you might be ignoring or have yet to take advantage of?

Are you negotiating for what you're worth? How can you do better?

How are you navigating office politics, conflicts, or difficult situations in your career? What can you do better? Whom do you need support or guidance from?

How do you handle feedback, criticism, or constructive criticism? How can you improve your approach to this?

Reflect on these questions and lay out your answers to help you identify the steps you need to take to advocate for and prioritize yourself. It could be getting really clear about the career goals you need to take action on, finding and speaking with a mentor, getting comfortable with negotiating your next raise, salary, or business contract, introducing a new source of income, having difficult conversations, or calling out inappropriate behavior.

By being intentional and taking action, it will get easier and easier to take advantage of opportunities when they arise, even when fear rears its ugly head. When fear seems like it's taking over, remind yourself of your value and why you are worth it.

CHAPTER 34

Taking Leaps of Faith

You might not be certain that the next path is the right one, but you owe it to yourself to do your best, regardless. So trust your intuition but be strategic.

Taking a leap of faith can be scary and nerve-racking. But you can approach it intentionally, which will in turn help you make the best objective decisions to move forward. Here are some questions to help you think things through.

What opportunities or chances is your intuition telling you to take?

What fears are holding you back from chasing those opportunities? How can you counter each fear?

What are the pros and cons of each opportunity or chance?

How would they radically change your life if you pursued the opportunities?

What buffer or fallback plans can you put in place so you're better prepared to take the next steps?

Now is a great time to commit to believing in yourself. Make the decision that you will take advantage of the opportunities that will come your way. You may not be able to predict the outcome, but sometimes it's necessary to simply trust the process and take the leap.

CHAPTER 35

Empowering Others Despite the Naysayers

People may not always like what you have to say, but stand in your truth and remember your "why."

We all learn, get inspired by, and grow from hearing other people's stories. We also all have a story to share that can be positively impactful to other people in our lives and even far beyond. Here are some questions to help you reflect on your own story and how far you've come, regardless of what the naysayers may say or think.

What stories from other people have impacted your life the most?

What's a story or experience you can share that you know the people in your life will benefit from?

What's holding you back from sharing your story or experience?

Tell yourself why you should share it anyway.

Sometimes the fear of judgment gets in the way. But as you consider your experiences, focus on the positive impact your stories could have on others – this will outshine all the negativity. Challenge yourself to share your experiences and empower someone else to succeed.

CHAPTER **36**

Choosing
a Rich Partner

The idea of having a rich partner goes beyond money. They should be rich in values, character, and integrity.

Partnership in a relationship is incredibly important – and so is being true to yourself when it comes to whom you choose to be with, regardless of what other people think or their opinions about your relationship. Here are some questions to help you reflect on your ideal relationship.

Who is your ideal partner, and what qualities do they possess?

What values are most important to you in a relationship? What are your non-negotiables, and what are you willing to be flexible on?

If you're in a relationship, are you and your partner on the same page when it comes to each other's goals and ambitions? Are you tracking your progress on what you want to accomplish together?

If you aren't on the same page right now, how can you be intentional about getting on the same page? Be more communicative? Seek counseling?

What are you committed to doing to build a relationship that works for you both?

Remember, when it comes to relationships, you want to make the best decisions for yourself and for your personal peace of mind. Never settle for second best, because you are worthy of someone who truly honors and uplifts you. If you're single, set the bar high and look for a partner who possesses the qualities and values you wrote down in this section. If you're in a relationship, work to make sure you and your partner maintain the same values and life goals to achieve your joint dreams.

CHAPTER 37

Stepping Outside Your Comfort Zone

The crossroads and the challenges will always show up, but remember why you started what you started, and never forget who you are.

As you grow in your career, business, or personal life, stepping outside your comfort zone is necessary. Yes, it's scary. But this is where the magic happens. This is where you turn all those dreams and what-ifs into reality. Here are some questions to help you reflect on the opportunities that may be waiting for you just outside your comfort zone.

> **What opportunities have presented themselves to you that would require you to step outside your comfort zone? Did you take them on?**

If you did, how did you adjust to the discomfort? If you didn't, what specifically held you back?

Knowing what you know now, how can you better prepare to step outside your comfort zone to open the doors to new opportunities and achieve your goals?

One way to get comfortable with stepping outside your comfort zone is to create a list of questions to ask yourself each time you're presented with a new opportunity. Some of these questions could be:

- When I'm older, will I look back and wish I had pursued this opportunity?
- Am I hesitant to do it because I'm afraid to take the leap, or because I know it's not a good fit for me?
- What's the worst thing that could happen if I pursued this opportunity? What's the best thing that could happen?

CHAPTER 38

Beating
Imposter Syndrome

Prioritize the important things in your life, give yourself the grace to accept that doing your best is enough, and remind yourself why you're amazing.

Imposter syndrome is real, and when we experience it, it can be incredibly limiting. But it doesn't have to be. Here are some questions to help you reflect and get past it.

In what specific situations in your life has imposter syndrome reared its head, and how did you handle it? (Finances, career, business, relationships, etc.)

How do you approach the feeling of being an imposter or incapable today?

What actions can you take to help tackle any imposter syndrome you might feel in the future so you can continue to focus on achieving your goals?

While feeling imposter syndrome may not go away permanently, it doesn't have to limit you. Reflect on your accomplishments and successes so far, no matter how small you think they are. Reflect on every difficult situation and how you overcame them. Focus on the positive side of every situation you are presented with. Doing these things will remind you of how capable you are, regardless of what the little voice in your head is saying.

Remember, there's no perfect blueprint to living your life and doing your best to accomplish your goals. It's all about making it work in the best way you can, knowing that you have what it takes to succeed.

CHAPTER **39**

Celebrating Yourself

You work hard. Acknowledge yourself and celebrate your successes.

A s you journey through your life, it's important to recognize your personal accomplishments and applaud yourself for them. (It can be the ultimate confidence boost!) Here are some questions to help you reflect.

Do you acknowledge and celebrate your successes? If so, how do you do it?

What makes you most proud when you reflect on the different areas in your life today?

How can you do a better job of acknowledging yourself more often?

List 10 accomplishments or successes you're most proud of (no matter how small!). Refer back to this list when you need motivation.

1.

2.

3.

4.

5.

6.

7.

8.

9.

10.

Start keeping track of your accomplishments (in a journal or in the notes app on your phone) and remind yourself why you are deserving; you've worked hard. And remember, no wins are too small to celebrate. Progress is progress is progress.

CHAPTER **40**

Intentionally
Choosing to Prosper
Moving Forward

What are three main goals you want to accomplish over the next 12 months? List them here, along with the key actionable steps you need to get started. Keep this list of goals handy throughout the next year so you have a focus point.

Goal	Key action step
Your finances	
1.	
2.	
3.	
Your career	
1.	
2.	
3.	

Goal	Key action step
Your side hustle/business	
1.	
2.	
3.	
Dealing with imposter syndrome	
1.	
2.	
3.	
Stepping out of your comfort zone to achieve your dreams and goals	
1.	
2.	
3.	
Other : _____	
1.	
2.	
3.	

CHAPTER 41

You Did It!

Congratulations on completing *your* **wealth plan**! You've taken a significant step toward financial freedom and prosperity. Remember, wealth is not just about money; it's about living a life that truly reflects your values, passions, and goals. You've shown up for yourself, done the work, and now have a clear roadmap to guide you toward your dreams.

As you close this workbook, remember that your wealth journey is just beginning. You have the power to create the life you desire, and every decision you make from this moment forward is a step toward that reality. Keep pushing forward, stay committed to your goals, and know that prosperity is yours for the taking. You can come back at any time to review, reassess, and even edit this workbook as necessary. So keep it handy!

Now, go out there and create the wealth, life, and legacy you deserve!

Index

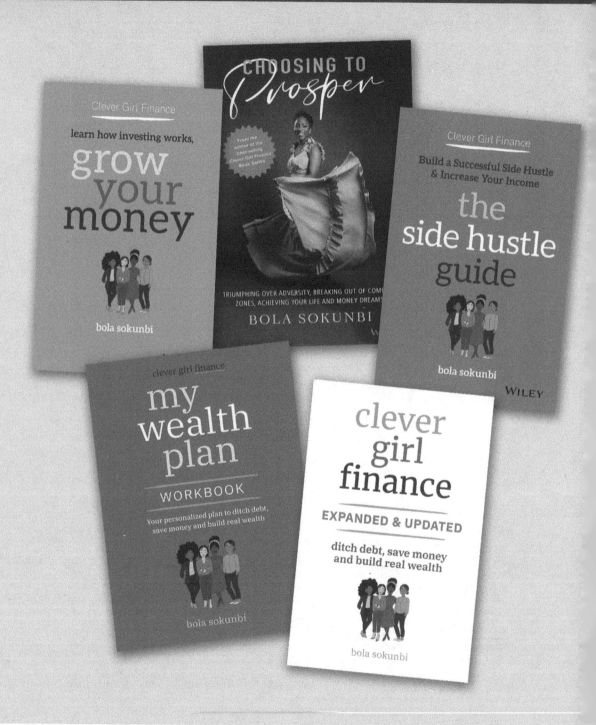